Whisky

Strathisla Distillery.

a Wee Guide to
Whisky

Euan Mitchell

GOBLINSHEAD

Musselburgh

a Wee Guide to Whisky

© Martin Coventry 1999
Published by GOBLINSHEAD
130B Inveresk Road
Musselburgh EH21 7AY
Scotland
tel 0131 665 2894; *fax* 0131 653 6566; *email* goblinshead@sol.co.uk

British Library Cataloguing in Publication Data
A catalogue record for this book is available from the British Library.

ISBN 1 899874 15 1

Typeset by GOBLINSHEAD using Desktop Publishing

WEE GUIDES
William Wallace
The Picts
Scottish History
The Jacobites
Robert Burns
Mary, Queen of Scots
Robert the Bruce
Haunted Castles of Scotland
Old Churches and Abbeys of Scotland
Castles and Mansions of Scotland
New for 1999
Prehistoric Scotland
Macbeth and Early Scotland
Whisky
Also published
The Castles of Scotland 2E (£14.50)
Haunted Places of Scotland (£7.50)
The Hebrides (£5.95)
William Wallace – Champion of Scotland (£6.95)

a Wee Guide to
Whisky

Contents

List of Illustrations

Acknowledgements

Thanks to many people and organisations for their help and co-operation in answering our queries, phone calls, faxes in providing the information for this book. In particular Joyce Miller, Martin Coventry, Frank McHardy at Springbank, Caroline Boyd and Gordon Muir. We would also like to acknowledge and thank the following for providing illustrations of their distilleries, shops or product.

- Ardbeg • Bladnoch • Cadenhead's • Edradour • Glen Moray
- Loch Fyne Whisky Shop • Macallan.

- United Distillers and Vintners for: Blair Athol; Caol Ila; Cardhu; Clynelish; Dalwhinnie; Glenkinchie; Glen Ord; Lagavulin; Royal Lochnagar; Talisker.

- Highland Distillers for Bunnahabhain and Black Bottle.

- J & G Grant for Glenfarclas.

- William Grant & Sons for Glenfiddich.

- Chivas Brothers for: Glen Grant; Glenlivet; Strathisla; spirit safe and washback, Strathisla; loading casks for export; barley.

- Stuart Andrew, Kintyre Photography for Springbank illustrations.

- JBB (Greater Europe) Plc for Tomintoul.

- Martin Coventry for Bowmore; Corgarff Castle; Colbost Museum Skye; Craighouse, Jura; Highland stream; Tobermory Bay, Mull.

- David Reed for Dallas Dhu.

- Joyce Miller for view of Arran.

How to Use the Book

This book is divided into two sections:

- The first section (pages 1-30) describes the history (pages 3-10), the process of whisky making (pages 11-21), and the taste and smell of whisky (pages 22-30).

- The second section (pages 31-84) lists more than 50 distilleries and other sites which can be visited or should be of interest. The section begins with the map (pages 32-33) which locates every site, and there is also a list of all the sites (page 34). The gazetteer is listed alphabetically (from page 35). Each entry begins with the name of the distillery, its location, and its reference on the map (pages 32-33). This is followed by a description of the distillery with notes about the whiskies produced there. The final part lists opening times with telephone, fax, email and web; and facilities, including parking, refreshments, sales area, admission charge, WC, and disabled access where available. Admission charges are as follows: £ = £3.50 or under; ££ = £3.50-£5.00; £££ = more than £5.00. There are some more places of interest at the end of this part (pages 79-84).

An index concludes the book (pages 85-86).

Warning

While the information in this book was believed to be correct at time of going to press – and was checked, where possible, with the visitor attractions – opening times and facilities, or other information, may differ from that included. All information should be checked with the visitor attractions before embarking on any journey. Inclusion in the text is no indication whatsoever that a site is open to the public or that it should be visited.

The inclusion or exclusion of a distillery, museum or other visitor attraction in the text should not be considered as a comment or judgement on that attraction.

Locations on the map are approximate.

Introduction

Whisk(e)y of one variety or another is produced in several locations around the world. However, it is the country of Scotland that remains synonymous with this drink in the hearts and minds of many people. While arguments rage as to its origins, there is little doubt it is the distilleries of Scotland that offer the greatest diversity of this noble spirit.

Essentially a very simple product, malt whisky, which is the focus of this guide, is based upon three ingredients: malted barley, water and yeast. Yet through a meticulous blend of skill and experience, not to mention the dramatic role played by the Scottish climate, each of the distilleries throughout Scotland creates a product that is quite simply unique.

The image of malt whisky may have suffered recently from its association with the more mature, affluent male drinker. For some younger drinkers this branding has been a negative influence and one which the industry is attempting to rectify. In some European countries, notably France, Spain, Portugal and Greece, as well as Venezuela and South Africa, the drinking of whisky, as a blend and with mixers, has become popular with the younger generation. In general terms whisky accounts for 16 of the world's 100 top-branded spirits and is the third biggest spirit consumed after gin and vodka. As a product it earns the country billions in export and provides direct or related employment for 60,000 people. As the eighth most important industry in Scotland, it brings benefits both to individuals and local communities alike, as well as pleasure for the consumer.

The Wee Guide to Whisky is designed to provide an insight into this fascinating subject both for the uninitiated and whisky converts, new and old. The first part of the book details the origins of the whisky industry in Scotland and outlines the production process, from malting of the barley to the finished article. The second part is a comprehensive guide to those distilleries which are currently open to the public, listing full contact details and access.

The malt whisky distilleries of Scotland form a striking image in their respective environments and are a great testimony to an industry that is an integral part of Scotland's past, present and future. Go and see them!

EM, Campbeltown, April 1999

a *Wee Guide* to
Whisky

The History of Whisky

Whisky has been made in Scotland for over 500 hundred years but nobody knows where, when and by whom the first distillation took place. There is one tradition that suggests that whisky, along with Christianity, was introduced to the Highlands by the Irish as early as the sixth or seventh century AD. However spores have been found on the island of Rum, off the west coast of Scotland, during an archeological investigation, which may suggest that some form of alcoholic drink was being made as early as 4000 BC. The earliest written reference to distilling is found in the Scottish Exchequer Rolls where an entry from 1494 notes *'eight bolls of malt to Friar John Cor wherewith to make aquavitae'*. A boll was an old Scots measure and eight of them weighed well over 1000 kg – enough to make over 400 bottles of whisky! *Aqua vitae* is Latin for water of life. The French *eau-de-vie* has the same meaning. The Gaelic translation, allowing for various spellings, is *uisge-beatha*, pronounced 'oosh-ki-bea-a'. This became *uskie* and, eventually, whisky.

During the next 300 years whisky distilling became extremely popular in Scotland for a number of reasons. Whisky was made, in the first instance, to drink. Water supplies in some areas were not very clean, and tea and coffee were very expensive, and outwith the pocket of much of the population. Whisky, and other home-brewed alcohol, was the acceptable daily liquid refreshment, for all ages: children and adults. Elizabeth Grant of Rothiemurchus describes the ubiquitous drinking of whisky in her memoirs. *'...We children were extremely fond of the tastes we got everywhere, particularly when the dram was well spiced and sweetened...'*. Secondly, without the modern technology of temperature and humidity-controlled grain stores, it was difficult to keep barley fresh and mould-free over the winter. As ambient temperature fluctuates grains of barley expand and contract and release moisture, which then settles on the grain, creating the right conditions for mould to grow. But converting the barley into whisky provided the population with a perfect product: it provided liquid refreshment and would keep over the winter. Most whisky at this time was actually made for private domestic consumption, although a commercial market gradually developed and a number of distilleries were granted licences.

By 1579 whisky making was widespread throughout the whole of Scotland. An Act of Parliament was passed in that year which complained about food shortages being caused because so much malt was being used in the distilling process. In 1644 the Scots Parliament imposed the first tax on whisky. The tax was later reduced by Oliver Cromwell and abolished on the restoration of Charles II in 1660.

Distilling was done on small, private stills and produced modest amounts of spirits which were used, on the most part, for personal consumption. Nevertheless, although officially selling the spirit produced from these stills was illegal, the authorities found it difficult to control both its retail and production. The quality of the whisky produced from the seventeeth until the nineteenth century was extremely varied and inconsistent, and often not all that pleasant. Some of these early spirits were sweetened and flavoured with herbs and spices, not simply to make them palatable for young children, as remembered by Elizabeth Grant, but also drinkable for adults.

The Act of Union in 1707 joined the parliaments of Scotland and England. A tax on malt – effectively a tax on alcohol – which was to be controlled by the Board of Excise was introduced in Scotland at only half the English rate. One of the notable provisions in the Act of Union specified that no tax on malted barley would be introduced while England was at war with France. The government tried to extend the English duty on ordinary malt – equivalent to one penny per bushel – to Scotland in 1713, but did not succeed in implementing it until 1725, and with somewhat mixed results. There were widespread riots against this extended tax, particularly at Shawfield, near Glasgow. The house of Daniel Campbell, the local M.P., was attacked and looted but with no obvious outcome as the unpopular tax remained in place.

Legal and illegal distilling

This marked the start of 100 turbulent years for Scots whisky makers – legal or not. The Union of 1707 was not a union of two equal powers and, due to England's greater size and power, Scotland and its government was ultimately subsumed and marginalised. Legislation from London either ignored the Scottish dimension totally or focused on it separately, apart from the rest of the country. This distant attitude could, on occasion, work to the benefit of the Scots. The Gin Act of 1736 was intended to reduce drunkenness in England by introducing heavy taxation on gin. The rather canny Scots took advantage of this, and subsequently increased export of whisky to their southern neighbour. By the early 1750s, the official annual production of whisky was over half a million gallons, and much of it was sold in England. After repeated crop failures between 1757 and 1760, the government banned commercial distilling throughout the whole of the United Kingdom for three years. Private distilling for personal use, however, was still allowed and, despite the government's policy, some of this 'private' supply managed to find its way to an enthusiastic black market in England. Distilling for private consumption was eventually made illegal in 1781, but continued for many years. Indeed, illicit stills were not brought under control until well into the nineteenth century.

At the same time as domestic stills were being rooted out and demolished many large-scale, commercial distilleries were established. By the mid-1780s the official trade had recovered from the barley shortages, and by 1786 over one million gallons of whisky was being sold to England. This flood of whisky from the north obviously did not please the London-based gin distillers, and they were better placed to lobby the government at Westminster about their concerns. As a result prohibitively high taxes were introduced on spirits sent from Scotland to England. This was followed, in 1778, by an act which required Scots to give one full year's notice if they intended to export

Corgarff Castle.

whisky to England. These rather off-putting bureaucratic hurdles certainly affected the commercial distillers' trade but had little effect on illegal distilling. This had continued to be carried out throughout the country, despite the presence of troops and excise men who were employed to police the situation. Troops were billeted in barracks where available; but castles, including the castle at Corgarff in Aberdeenshire, were also used to house soldiers during the eighteenth century. Excise men were extremely unpopular with the ordinary population. One of Scotland's more famous excise men was Robert Burns, probably better known for his poetry! Burns acknowledged how unpopular and dangerous the job of 'gauger' or measurer was, although he certainly appeared to have carried out his duties with diligence. He recorded public opinion about gaugers in the song *The De'il's awa wi' the Excise man*.

> *We'll mak our maut and we'll brew our drink,*
> *We'll laugh, sing and rejoice, man*
> *And mony braw thanks to the meikle black deil,*
> *That danc'd awa wi' the Excise man*

Excise and tax

The whole excise situation was quite shambolic and remained so until 1820 when the Duke of Gordon put forward a proposal to the govern-

Colbost Croft Museum, Skye – there is a replica still at the museum.

ment. He suggested that landowners could help stamp out illicit distilling in return for more acceptable levels of taxation. Up to that point many landowners had turned a blind eye to illegal distilling by their tenants, as they had benefited from the process along with their tenants. Many tenants, with few other means of generating income, used any revenue gained from their distilling to help pay their rents, and so provided their landlords with some ready cash. However, to ensure the cooperation of the landowners it was guaranteed that they would not lose out financially from this new arrangement. Their taxes were reduced and, at the same time, they still received rents from their tenants. It was the tenants who had to find the necessary cash from other sources.

Following the introduction of the Excise Act of 1823 illegal whisky production finally waned, although legal distilling continued to flourish and increase. In the years 1822 and 1823 14,000 illicit stills were seized. However it was not until 1860 that illegal distilling ceased to be a problem for the authorities. The excise men and the landlords had finally managed to eliminate virtually all illicit stills, leaving the way clear for the rise of commercial whisky distilling.

Commercial whisky distilling

Until the nineteenth century, whisky was distilled twice in pot stills; but much of the spirit produced was of inconsistent quality. It took time to produce but, with skill and experience, a rich flavoursome spirit could be obtained – although not on every occasion. Most whisky was sold in casks to grocer shops and wine merchants. These shop keepers created their own mixes in order to overcome the problems of quality and quantity.

In 1826 a new kind of still was patented by Robert Stein of Kilbagie in Clackmannanshire that revolutionised whisky making in Scotland. The new equipment could distil continuously, rather than in batches, and as only one distillation was required the whole process was much quicker. Five years later Aeneas Coffey, from Dublin, brought out an even better version. Coffey's still produced high-strength, cheap spirit, but the product by itself did not have much flavour. The type of whisky produced by Coffey was grain whisky. Nevertheless merchants, with an eye for a commercial opportunity, tried mixing more expensive malt whisky with cheaper grain whisky, and so the resultant product, known as blended whisky, was created. At present blended whisky accounts for almost 95% of all Scotch whisky sold. The other 5% is, however, the real stuff – malt whisky.

During the 1860s a disaster struck the vineyards of Europe which was to prove a huge boon for Scottish whisky producers. A species of beetle – the *phylloxera* – which attacks the roots of vines was accidentally introduced from America. American vines were resistant to the *phylloxera*, but European ones were not. The destruction of the vineyards meant no wine production and, more importantly, no brandy. Some time later the vine growers discovered that American vine roots could be grafted onto their own vines to provide protection, but in the meantime Scottish whisky producers capitalised on a this timely opportunity. The lack of wine and brandy meant there was a gap in the market. The continuous still produced whisky quickly and cheaply, and by flavouring it with malt whisky, commercial distillers had an ideal product. Blended whisky is lighter in taste than malt whisky. At the time the Scotch whisky producers themselves actually attributed the huge increase in whisky sales to the theory that the lighter blended whisky was more suited to the southern palate than stronger malt whisky, rather than because of the more prosaic *phylloxera* epidemic.

The ups and downs of the 20th century

The *phylloxera* boom ended in the mid 1890s, when brandy and wine came back onto the market; and as a result many commercial producers of whisky went out of business. One of the most prominent of these companies was the flamboyant Pattisons of Leith. When the company folded it had debts of over £500,000. Pattisons was well-known for its extreme marketing ploys; one campaign involved training 500 parrots to repeat *'drink Pattison's whisky'*. The parrots were then circulated throughout Edinburgh. However, as they later went out of business, perhaps their advertising campaigns had more style than their commercial viability.

Casks being prepared for export.

The renewed competition from European spirits in the early years of the twentieth century also coincided with a fall in domestic consumption. During the 1830s the average consumption of spirits in proof gallons was 2.55 per head of population. By the 1930s this had fallen to 0.35 per head. This drop in consumption was due to several factors: economic depression, over production, and the influence of the Temperance Movement. The leading Scottish Temperance figures were John Dunlop and William Collins. Both individuals produced pamphlets and travelled widely, during the 1820s and 1830s, delivering lectures on the perils of alcohol. Most of the reformers were against the drinking of spirits, but total abstinence from all alcohol was also important for some. The Temperance Movement was influential throughout the late-nineteenth and early-twentieth centuries, and their campaigns resulted in reduced licensing hours by 1853. Alcohol and poverty were portrayed together as the major ills of society. Later temperance became an important political issue for all the major parties, although full prohibition, as carried out in the United States, was rejected.

Another contributory factor to the decline was the fact that the malt whisky-making capacity was too great for the available market. Inevitably many distilleries closed. By this time the market was almost entirely for blended whisky – no distiller seriously tried to market malt whisky as a single product. Those businesses which remained struggled to stay afloat.

The next 70 years, indeed, were not particularly successful for the malt whisky industry. Two world wars, coupled with a period of economic depression, did not provide the ideal trading conditions for luxury products like malt whisky: sales of scotch whisky during this time were dominated by the blended brands.

During the First World War the prime minister, Lloyd George, believed that too much drinking was hampering the war effort. In order to combat this problem he introduced a number of measures such as the Immature Spirits Act of 1915. Whisky straight from the still – 'New make' whisky – certainly did not appeal to everyone, but it was very cheap which made it popular. The Immature Spirits Act made it illegal to sell whisky until it had been matured for at least three years, thus the selling of new make whisky was prohibited. Also until this point whisky was usually bottled at a cask strength of 60% alcohol by volume. Most people drank it 'half and half with lots of water'! The government asked the distillers to reduce the strength to 30%. The distillers did not want this, so a compromise was reached and the level was fixed at 40%. Another measure which attempted to reduce the amount of alcohol drunk was the banning of the custom known as 'treating'. Treating was the buying a round of drinks for friends, but instead customers were only allowed to buy drink for themselves.

After the rationing of barley during the Second World War ended it was still some years before stocks could be built up. Whisky was, and is, a valuable export product and, in order that the export market could be filled first, a quota system was used. This regulated the proportion of scotch allocated for the home market and the quota system was used until 1959. Although ensuring enough whisky was available for export, this system resulted in a limited growth in the domestic market.

It was always possible to buy malt whisky during these years, but it was not bottled by the people who produced it. A number of independent bottlers were malt whisky's lifeline, although often a precarious one. These companies would buy casks of malt whisky, mature it, then bottle it for retail. Gordon & MacPhail Ltd. of Elgin and Cadenhead's from Campbeltown are the two oldest, and best known, independent bottling companies.

Why did most distillers concentrate on selling blended whisky rather than single malts? One explanation was the one used by the distillers themselves: that malt whisky was too powerfully flavoured for most palates. Certainly the boom years up to 1895 would seem to support this view. Blended whisky was freely available and sold well. This was in part due to the absence of brandy from the market. Another factor was the time and cost of producing malt whisky. Almost all the malts sold in the country are at least ten years old: stocks have to be laid down to mature for this time before they can be marketed. Therefore there is no immediate return on the cost of production and storage. Because of post-war economic anxieties it was not until 1954, at the earliest, that distillers could plan ahead with any feeling of security. Without financial security, both for the distillers and their customers, mass marketing of malt whisky was regarded as too risky.

However, in 1963, nine years later, William Grant & Sons, makers of Glenfiddich, was the first company to start marketing malt whisky; first to the old traditional market of England and then to the rest of the world. It is still the biggest world-wide seller. These days almost all the best malts are bottled at, and by, their own distillers, often at several different ages. There are also still several independent bottlers, including MacPhails and Cadenhead's, who bottle and market different malts at different ages and from different types of storage casks.

The Process of Whisky Making

Malting

Making malt whisky is not a difficult process. For years crofters made whisky without the benefits of modern technology, although the quality of the spirit they distilled may not have as refined as today's product. Today making malt whisky is as much an art as a science. The modern product reaches a quality controlled standard because of the use of science, but the subtle nuances, and mixture of flavourings, is the result of the distillers' art and skill, particularly that of the stillman. Producing a perfect whisky every time is therefore not just a scientific equation, but a craft acquired with years of practice.

The ingredients and process used to make whisky are themselves simple enough. Barley, peat, water and yeast. A pair of stills, and some casks to mature the spirit in are all that is required. There are only six or seven steps involved. These are: malting, drying, milling, mashing, fermenting, distilling, maturing and, usually, vatting.

Malt whisky is always made from barley. Barley, in its natural state, will not ferment and so it is malted first. The barley seed has two main parts: the small seed which will grow into a new plant, and a larger food store that the seedling draws on until its roots and leaves are established. It is this food store which is needed for whisky. The starch in the food store does not itself ferment, but as the seed starts to grow the starch is converted into sugars, which do.

The barley needs to be soaked for a few days until it starts to grow and begin converting starch into sugar. The malting process is then halted, in order to prevent the seedling using up all the sugar. Although not all the starch is converted into sugar at this stage, the barley also produces

Barley.

Barley is spread over the floor of the kiln and heated and raked.

enzymes. These are organic catalysts, called diatase, which in solution can continue to convert starch into sugar even after the barley itself is dead.

The barley is killed off by drying it out. Traditionally the drying was carried out by burning peat under the 'green malt'. The barley was spread over the floor of the kiln and heated and raked, for several days. This not only dried out the malt, but smoked it as well. This smoking results in the pronounced peat smoke flavour found in the finished product. Peat is still found on some parts of the Highlands and Islands of Scotland, although supplies are dwindling. Most of the peat used in distilleries these days is imported. The peat-burning kiln traditionally has a pagoda-shaped vent, a feature which helps identify different distilleries. Although most distillers do not do their own malting now, a lot of distilleries still have these recognisable vents.

Peat consists of undecomposed and compressed vegetation, mainly sphagnum moss. It also includes sedges, rushes and reeds. The climatic conditions in north Europe, in other words the temperature and rainfall, resulted in organic matter accumulating faster than it could decompose and so resulted in the formation of peat. The quality of the water is also important to the creation of peat: ideally acidic with low oxygen and nutrient levels.

Sphagnum thrives in these conditions. It does not fix oxygen easily, as it actually increases the acidity of the water, and so any oxygen in the falling rain is used by the growing moss, and does not permeate down past the surface plant. Sphagnum can also absorb many times its own weight in liquid. This, combined with its lack of bacteria, results in an almost completely sterile environment, and because of this sterility it was often used to dress bleeding wounds, even during the First World War – and also as an early toilet paper. Peat was, and is still, used as a domestic fuel. When it is first cut it contains 90% water, and so it requires much drying out before it can be used as a burning fuel. It is cut out of the moor during the early summer, and left to dry in the wind and sun before it is brought down to the home and stacked up for the winter. It is a very labour-intensive job, involving all family and community members. Recently manual peat cutting using flauchters and taskers – turf and peat-cutting spades – which cut the peat

Kiln, Springbank Distillery.

into blocks has been replaced by machine cutting, which cuts the peat into sausage-shaped bricks. When burnt, peat provides about two-thirds of the heat as the same weight of coal. However, peat is used for the distinctive peat-smoke flavour it gives whisky rather than for its thermal qualities.

Traditionally every distillery would malt its own barley, but due to economies of scale currently most malting is carried out in a few large commercial malting plants. These plants will produce different batches of malt to the exact specification of each distiller. The most obvious difference in malting are the levels, and length, of peat smoking required for each distillery. Most distillers, apart from those on Islay, now use lightly-smoked malt, and some even use unsmoked malt. This difference is clearly reflected in the taste of the different whiskies.

Milling

The next stage is the milling of the malted barley. It is ground into a coarse flour, called grist, to enable the sugars and other flavours to dissolve out more easily in the next process: mashing. Most mills use two sets of rollers: the first set is designed to crack the husks of the malt without grinding it. The malt then passes through a system of beaters, which separate the husks from the corn, and then the whole lot goes through a finer set of rollers. These grind the grist into a flour, but still leave the husks more or less intact. The barley needs to be ground fairly finely so that the sugars and starches can be dissolved, but leaving the husks intact makes it easier to drain out after mashing.

Mashing

The next ingredient which is added is water, and the quality of water is one of the factors which affects the flavour and style of the finished whisky. The water in the south-east of Britain is hard, but further north it becomes much softer. Rainwater is naturally soft, but as it percolates through rock it becomes harder because it picks up minerals. In the area south of Humber and Dorset the rock is chalky and full of limestone. As water passes through chalk and limestone it picks up calcium and magnesium carbonates. With so many minerals already dissolved in and flavouring the hard water, the subtle flavours from the malted barley would be difficult to absorb. In contrast, the water in Scotland, especially in the Highland area, is very soft, often already peat-flavoured, and is slightly acidic. As there are very few impurities dissolved in it, this water can easily absorb the flavour of the malted barley, along with the sugars and small quantities of naturally-occurring essential oils that all add to the overall flavour of whisky.

With so much of Scotland lacking naturally-occurring lime, the soil is lower in fertility. Those varieties of plants which tolerate these conditions naturally are therefore extremely hardy. In order to compensate for this shortage, sea shells were burnt in order to produce lime. Throughout the country there are derelict lime kilns where lime was produced to increase crop productivity. In the north and west areas of Scotland it is possible to see a profusion of naturally growing wild flowers in areas known as machair land. These are lime-rich grassland next to sandy beaches, where the lime comes naturally from the sand and shells. In any of the Hebridean islands, or on coastal areas throughout Scotland, it is very easy to identify these machair lands.

During the mashing process hot water is added to the grist. Hot, but not boiling, as this would de-nature the diastase and stop it converting the starch into sugar. The water runs through into the mashing machine, a copper tube with a rotating screw inside it, and mixed with the grist. Either three or four waters are added to the mash tun, with each water progressively hotter than the previous one. The first two waters, known as wort, carry the bulk of the sugar extracted from the grist and are pumped through a cooler to the fermentation vessel, known as a washback. During the draining of the three to four waters through the grist, about 75% of the weight is extracted. The remaining 25% – the draff – is dried and normally used as animal feed.

Fermentation

The first two waters from each mash are cooled and combined with yeast in large washbacks for the next process: fermentation. Traditional wooden washbacks are made of larch or Oregon pine and are the shape of large half-casks set upright. Many distillers have moved over to stainless steel as it is easier to maintain and clean. It is possible to see traditional washbacks in Scotland being used in a somewhat unusual manner. In the village of Findhorn, near Forres, second-hand washbacks have been upturned and converted into houses.

Yeast are micro-organisms, which in the right environment of moisture, food, oxygen and temperature can multiply extremely rapidly. Yeast feeds on the sugar in the wash, and produces alcohol – predominantly ethanol and CO_2 – as a by-product. There is a huge variety of species of yeast, but the species used for making whisky is *Saccaromyces Cerevisiae*. Different strains of this will produce slightly different results. Some ferment more quickly or produce higher alcohol yields. Others give more complex flavours. Most distillers use a mixture of yeasts to achieve an optimum balance. They often include a proportion of brewer's yeast as well, as the combination seems to give higher spirit yields.

The level of nitrogen in

Washback at Strathisla Distillery.

the barley can be a problem for distillers. Too much nitrogen means that there will be higher protein levels in the malt. This encourages yeast growth at the expense of alcohol production. To avoid this problem it is important that farmers, who sell to maltsters, do not use too much fertiliser on their crops.

Fermentation usually occurs quite quickly, in about 40 to 48 hours, and the solution produced is known as wash. This solution is between 6% and 9% alcohol by volume. In the summer, with higher ambient temperatures, the fermentation can progress too quickly and some of the subtle flavour can be lost. Most wine producers face similar problems and so artificially control the temperature during fermentation in order to retain maximum freshness and flavour. High temperature is usually only a problem for distillers in Scotland during July and August. This, coupled with less water being available during these months, is the reason why most distillers cease production in the middle of the summer.

Distillation

The wash is then distilled, usually twice, to increase the alcohol strength to approximately 68.5%. It is during distilling that the quality and taste of the product is really achieved. Distilling is a method of separating two liquids by taking advantage of their different boiling points. Alcohol boils at a lower temperature than water, so when the wash is boiled the first part to evaporate contains a higher proportion of alcohol. This evaporated liquid can then be condensed, and collected, by cooling the vapour. The vapour is usually condensed into liquid as it passes through spiral copper tubes

Stills, Springbank Distillery.

immersed in cold water. Most malt whiskies have usually been distilled twice. The product of the first distillation is usually about 24% alcohol and is known as the low wines. The liquid is distilled again, in a smaller still, and part of the second distillation is collected in the spirit receiver as spirit at between 69 and 71% alcohol by volume.

The stills themselves are enclosed copper pots, with a tube at the top called a lye pipe to take the vapour to the condenser. Copper is used as it is an easy metal to work into shape. All distillers use copper as it plays an important part in the development of the flavours in the spirit. Experiments with cheaper and more durable stainless steel stills have been tried, but rejected, as the resultant spirit was not of the same quality as that achieved using copper. Small amounts of copper are dissolved in the spirit during distillation and, as well as acting as a catalyst in the formation of flavoursome esters, copper also suppresses levels of undesirable sulphur compounds in the finished spirit.

The size and shape of the stills also appear to have a marked effect on the style of the spirit in a way that is not understood. In general a tall-necked still will produce a cleaner, lighter tasting spirit than the oilier, fruitier character produced from a shorter-necked still. As it passes up the neck of the still the vapour begins to cool. It is not pure alcohol vapour, but a mixture containing some of the natural oils from the barley. These oils condense at a lower temperature than alcohol. With a high-necked still, the oils cool enough to recondense before they reach the top of the neck, and so fall back into the still. The spirit leaving the condenser in a tall-necked still will not be as oily as the spirit produced from a short-necked still. The different shapes of still do not produce better or worse spirits, just distinct flavours. A lighter spirit will allow the malty character to shine through, whereas an oily spirit will result in a fruitier whisky. However whatever the reason or result, most distillers are reluctant to change

Stillman, Strathisla Distillery.

the size or shape of their stills, in case they lose one of the characteristics of their whisky.

The stills are not the only variables in the whisky making process. Operation of the still depends on human skill and experience. From the second distillation the stillman separates out from the spirit still three distinct parts of each run. The first part of the run is known as the foreshots. These contain the concentrated, naturally-produced, higher alcohols. Their inclusion in the drinking spirit would give the imbiber a severe headache. The next part of the run is the middle cut. This is the bit that is collected as spirit and will become drinkable whisky. Finally, the third part, or feints, is run off. These, like the foreshots, are also unusable in this form. The foreshots and fients are added to the next batch of low wines to be redistilled in the second distillation. There is some lee-way in the size and nature of the middle cut. Different distilleries take between 15 and 24% of the second distillation as their middle cut. The amount or timing of the middle cuts is important to the final flavour. They might be from nearer the foreshots, producing a light spirit, or down towards the fients, resulting in an oilier one.

Maturation

The new spirit is then watered down slightly to 63% and at this stage it is put into oak casks to mature. The whisky is still relatively crude at this stage, but during its years in cask the maturing spirit will lose any rough edges, pick up flavours from the wood and develop in complexity. Each year around 2% of each cask evaporates – the Angel's share – so the longer a whisky is matured the less of it there is, and the more expensive it becomes. However as the wood expands and contracts over the years other environmental influences are absorbed into the whisky, such as pine, seaweed and sea salt.

Oak casks are used, but never new oak. Some alcohol, such as red and white wine, benefits from time spent in new oak. But these wines seldom spend more than a year in new oak, and their lower alcoholic strength does not leach out the flavours from the wood so quickly. Most malt whisky spends at least 10 years in cask, and if new oak was used it would give an overwhelmingly woody character to the whisky. Therefore casks that have been used before, mainly in the maturation of bourbon whiskey in America or sherry in Spain are used.

To complicate matters further American oak has a denser structure than European oak, which also affects not only how quickly the whisky will mature, but also the cost of making the casks. Because they are cheaper many American oak casks are used to mature sherry. However, the European oak being less dense then the American variety, breathes more easily, allowing the spirit to mature at a faster rate. It is also more resiny and adds slightly different flavours to the spirit than American oak. Both types add vanilla notes to the spirit, as they both contain compounds known as vanillins: the aromatic principle of vanilla. The type of wood a whisky is matured in also influences its overall flavour.

Oak, like any wood, is made up of tiny tubes. The tubes in European oak are larger than those in American oak. If a saw is used to cut European oak it is possible that these tubes will be cut through on the diagonal. If the staves of a cask are cut like this, some of the ends would be in contact with the maturing spirit and allow some of the spirit to leak out. To counter this, European oak is therefore split by hand along the grain of the wood. With the denser American oak it is possible to machine cut the staves. Hand splitting is, of course, more expensive and labour intensive, and there is more wastage. Both kinds of casks have their advantages and disadvantages in terms of cost, and their effects on the flavour, of the whisky.

American whiskey, by law, has to be matured in new oak. The legislation was introduced in America to protect the jobs of the coopers who make the casks. American whiskey, apart from using different grain and being matured for fewer years than its Scottish relative, has a very

Casks, Springbank.

different flavour –
almost as if maple syrup
has been added – as a
result of maturing in
new oak casks.
However the benefit to
Scottish whisky makers
of American whiskey
makers having to use
only new casks is a
financial one. It is
expensive to make
casks and as they can
only use them once the
used casks are bought
by Scottish distillers at
a much reduced price.
American whiskey takes
a lot of character and
flavour from the wood,
but there is still some
life in it by the time it is
used for Scottish whisky.

Casks, Springbank.

Using an American whiskey cask will give a distinct vanilla edge, but it is
not such a strong flavour that the malt flavour is lost. On the other
hand American oak is denser than Spanish oak, so the whisky matures
more slowly, which is also beneficial.

Spanish casks will have usually been used in the making the rich,
dark oloroso sherries. Traditionally sherry was shipped to Britain in
casks and bottled here, giving distillers a cheap source of casks.
However since the early 1980s sherry has been bottled in Spain, so
these days distillers have to source these casks directly from the
Spanish. An oloroso sherry cask will give far more flavour and colour to
the whisky than a bourbon one. A dark coloured malt that smells of
toffee and raisins will almost certainly have been matured in a sherry
cask. Each cask will be used three to four times, but each time it has
less left to contribute to the character of the whisky. Usually it is only
the contents of first or second fill casks that are bottled as single malts.

Vatting

In practice most of the mainstream malts will be the product of a vatting together, or blending, or the contents of many different casks in order to ensure consistency of flavour from batch to batch. A few will use all sherry, some will use all bourbon, and many will use a proportion of both. And distillers will not necessarily use the same proportions in the vattings of the different ages of their whiskies. In the 18 year old Glenlivet, for example, the sherry influence is far more obvious than in the 12 year old. Increasingly, single cask malts are being bottled for sale and are proving very popular.

Before most malts are bottled they are usually chill filtered. This is largely a cosmetic exercise which, unfortunately, removes something from the flavour of the whisky. An unfiltered whisky, especially an oily one, will go slightly cloudy with the addition of water. The flavoursome oily compounds dissolve in alcohol, but not in water. When the alcohol strength is reduced with the addition of water, some of the oiliness comes out of solution and causes cloudiness. Similarly, if an unfiltered whisky becomes too cold it will probably appear slightly cloudy, because a cold liquid cannot dissolve as much as a warm one. To avoid that slight cloudiness most distillers will filter out some of the oiliness from their whisky. A whisky that goes slightly cloudy on the addition of water is therefore usually a good sign. It is probably one that has not been chill filtered and so will retain all its original flavour. Springbank, from Campbeltown, does not chill filter its whiskies, contributing to their wonderful rich flavour.

To illustrate this difference, by smell and taste, the two official bottlings of 10 year old Laphroaig are a good contrast. The standard strength whisky is chill filtered, the cask strength is not. The standard strength Laphroaig is 40%, one of the fullest flavoured drams on the market. On the other hand the cask strength is 57% and retains its intense flavours even after the addition of water to dilute it to 40%. Because the improved flavour has proved popular with single malt afficionados many independent bottlings are now unfiltered.

The Taste and Smell of Whisky

Once a whisky has been bottled, as long as it is unopened, the flavour will remain the same for decades. Knowing a bit about its history, and how it is made, gives some background to the production of the spirit but does not explain the multitude of smells, flavours and colour of different whiskies. Describing the smells and tastes of any drink is a very subjective exercise. There is no unified language for tasting. Two people may use different words to describe exactly the same smell and taste, and both will be correct. Smell is a far more important and precise sense than taste. There are actually only four different tastes: salt, sweet, sour and bitter, although other 'tastes' are created as the fluid or food is warmed in the mouth. As these 'tastes' develop aromas filter through at the same time. However, more importantly, it is actually possible to distinguish thousands of smells. Smells have different levels: there are some overtones which are immediately apparent, but others may only appear later, as the whisky becomes more familiar. Undoubtedly first impressions are very important, but a whisky continues to reveal its secrets as it is nursed and sipped. The nosing of whisky is therefore an important part of its tasting. The aromatics and concentrates of a whisky are best drawn out with the addition of a small amount of soft water.

It is easier to smell differences and changes in smells, than to identify completely new ones. Whisky tastings are therefore not just an excuse to sample lots of different kinds, but are useful in learning how to identify differences between them. Trying a malt in isolation means assessing it on memory. With several malts it is possible to go back and forward, comparing the smells and tastes. This can help highlight differences and makes them easier to describe. If only one whisky is tasted it can often be difficult to describe but with two, or more, it becomes easier. There are five aspects to assessing the overall taste and quality of a whisky: the colour, the nose, the body, the palate and the finish. Colour can range from pale yellow to dark brown; the nose from gentle to smoky; the body may be light to full; the palate straightforward oak to complex spice and fruit, and the final finish may be delicately crisp and short to powerful and lingering.

The taste

In order to describe and identify taste and features of different whiskies there is a framework or a set of questions which can be used as a check list of features to note. The check list is quite similar to that used in wine tasting. For example: the variety of grape; which country or region it is from; has it been in wood; is it too young or too old; how much fruit or tannin does it have; what is the fruit/acidity balance? Obviously these exact questions do not all apply to whisky but a similar framework is usable. Six questions which are more appropriate to whisky are: How malty is it; what kind of casks has the whisky been matured in; how fruity; how smoky; has it any hint of the sea and finally how old is it? The headings used here may not be what professional tasters would use, but it should help the new amateur taster to develop their own tasting language.

Half of the distilleries in Scotland are located in the north-east of the country, between Inverness and Aberdeen, in what is known as the Speyside area. Some of the whiskies produced in this area will be used to help explain the headings, although others are also included. Although whiskies are obviously different, they are all on one broad spectrum, with lighter malty whiskies at one end, and richer sherry cask matured ones at the other.

How malty is the whisky?

Malted barley is one of the main ingredients in whisky and so it might be assumed that this would be the most prominent smell and taste. Maltiness is easiest to spot in whiskies like Glenlivet, Glen Grant or Glenfiddich. At their standard bottling ages there does not appear to be much sherry influence from the casks and so the malted character can shine through. However, the term 'maltiness' can cover a variety of malty notes; from strong and dominant to soft and gentle.

What type of cask was used?

The next most important influence on the flavour of whisky is the type of cask used. Vanillin and tannin compounds occur naturally in wood and give vanilla and caramel taste to the spirits stored in it. From bourbon wood or second fill sherry casks, the whisky is strongly flavoured with vanilla notes reminiscent of ice-cream, caramel and even coffee. New sherry casks give stronger toffee, raisins or chocolate flavours. Glenfarclas and Macallan are full of these flavours if they have been matured in sherry casks. When whisky comes off the still it is a colourless liquid and so it absorbs all its colour from the storage cask. Bourbon wood gives a light golden colour; sherry a darker brown one.

Does it taste of fruit?

The fruitiness of some malts is due to the presence of essential oils. Longmorn, for example, is one of the oiliest Speysides. One sip rolled around the mouth leaves an oiliness on the tongue. Rich fruit flavours are associated with this oiliness. In Longmorn's case there is a hint of sherry as well. Another aspect of fruitiness is found in those malts with a distinctly floral side.

How smoky is it?

Peat smoke does not play a such big part in Speyside these days, although there are still a few where smoky flavours are quite noticeable. Cragganmore, which has recently closed to the public, has a lovely flavoursome maltiness, a bit like straw and hay. But it also has a distinctly smoky edge which does not overpower the maltiness. Both of these flavours can be tasted and smelt but neither dominates.

How much sea air is there?

Often whiskies are noted for their seaweed or sea salt flavour. Around a quarter of the existing distilleries are situated at, or near, the coast and, as oak casks are slightly porous, they allow the contents to breathe. As they breathe the more volatile compounds are slowly lost, and at the same time some of the roughness of the new spirit. As this roughness is taken off other compounds react, as does the wood itself, to develop more complex flavours. 2% – the Angel's share – is lost through evaporation, and the empty space is filled with air from the environment. The salty sea air slowly permeates the casks and the whisky itself. Salt highlights and brings out flavours in all foods. Even puddings can taste sweeter with a hint of salt in them. The same is true for whisky – some of the hidden flavours are brought out because of the salty air. Springbank, from Campbeltown, is intensely fruity at any age, whether it has been stored in sherry casks or not, and also has a definite coconut edge. But it is in their older whiskies that the salt flavour finish is most obvious. It is both salty and sweet.

Salty freshness is one effect of the sea, the other is the reputed medicinal qualities associated with Islay malts. The prevailing wind in Scotland comes from the south-west. It travels across the Atlantic ocean, absorbing moisture as it passes over the sea, moisture which is, of course, dropped as soon as it meets the land on the west of the country. Iodine is present in small quantities in sea water, and so there is some iodine in this rain. Perhaps the medicinal qualities in Islay whiskies can be attributed to the iodine from the rain water. However there are other factors to consider as well. Whisky from five of the seven remaining distilleries on Islay which smoke barley quite strongly, are all strong in iodine char-

Ardbeg Distillery, Islay.

acter. This is not the case with the whisky from those which do not heavily smoke the barley. Peat acts as a filter and iodine builds up in it from the rain which has fallen over thousands of years. Therefore it is possible that the water and the peat, as well as the smoking contribute to the medicinal quality. This quality may also be why Islay malts are so controversial.

How old is it?

It might seem that the older the whisky is then the better it will be. This is not the case. Firstly, not all whiskies mature at the same rate. Rich oily ones take longer than lighter ones. Some of the lighter Lowland or Speyside whiskies will mature quickly, and are ready to drink after only eight or 10 years. However smoothness is not always the only goal. Talisker, from Skye, is a big, mouth-filling monster of a dram: rich and oily. At 10 years old it might appear that it needs more time to mature. But then it would lose the youthful exuberance that gives it so much impact. Hiding away under the smoke and slight iodine on the nose, is just a touch of raspberry. Raspberriness is often very obvious in any new spirit, but has usually disappeared before it is bottled.

Laphroaig, from Islay, is another good example. It is bottled by the distillers at 10 and 15 years. At 10 years old it is all smoky, iodiney and salty up front. But by 15 years it has mellowed; the smoke and iodine are less dominant, and by this age the maltiness and fruit come to the front. However few malts continue to improve much past 20 years. A very good malt, in a very good cask, will last longer, but for most whisky the woodiness from the cask will become increasingly dominant, until the wood taste overpowers the spirit.

Regional differences

Just as wines from different regions or countries have different characteristics, so do malt whiskies from the different regions of Scotland. The traditional regions for whisky production are: Lowland, Highland, Campbeltown and Islay. These days Speyside is usually regarded separately from the rest of the Highlands. In addition there are also whiskies produced on a few other Scottish islands. Knowing which area a malt was produced in can give an idea of its style and, perhaps, its quality.

Lowland

The lowland area covers the bottom third of Scotland; that is every-where south of a line between Dumbarton and Dundee. There are very few distilleries still open and producing whisky in this region; two malts which are commonly available are: Auchentoshan, produced in the west of Glasgow and Glenkinchie, produced south-east of Edinburgh. Glenkinchie, which produces a light whisky with a smooth, dry taste, can be visited but the only other lowland distillery which is open to the public is Bladnoch, near Wigtown, which used to produce a delicate sweet whisky. Auchentoshan is not open to the public. The Lowlands produce the lightest tasting malts. Prolonged storage in sherry casks

Bladnoch Distillery.

during maturation would swamp the delicate flavours of lowland malts, so it tends to be their soft maltiness that is their defining feature. They seem to capture the essences of the malted barley. Lowland malts may be light in style compared to some, but not in class or character.

Highland

This refers to everywhere north of the line between Dumbarton and Dundee, excluding Campbeltown, Speyside, and the islands. The whiskies produced in the Highlands tend to be more fully-flavoured than their Lowland counterparts. A few are light and malty, but most have a richer, fruitier character. There are also several coastal distilleries where the influence of the sea on the whisky is quite apparent. None of the mainstream bottlings from these distilleries are completely dominated by one wood type. Glenmorangie, a very popular delicate malt, is produced at Tain. Some of the whisky produced at Glenmorangie has been matured (finished) for a short time in either port, madeira or sherry wood. This process has rounded off the fruitiness of the whisky rather than overwhelm it with flavour. There are other malts from the eastern highlands, including Fettercairn, a light, sweet malt, and Royal Lochnagar, which has a medium-bodied taste with creamy overtones. And from Perthshire, Glengoyne distillery produces a light, smooth and fresh-nosed whisky, and Blair Athol a peaty, nutty 12 year old. All these distilleries are open to the public.

Campbeltown

The smallest of the malt whisky producing regions, the town of Campbeltown sits near the tip of the Mull of Kintyre: the peninsula jutting out to the south-west of Scotland. Although only two distilleries remain now, in the boom years of the late 1800s and 1900s there were 30 distilleries and it was the single most important town in Scotland for malt whisky production. Prohibition in the United States seems to have sounded the death knell for most of the Campbeltown distilleries. However although the legal market was lost, some distillers continued to export illegal supplies. The two remaining working distilleries, Springbank and Glen Scotia, produce very different products, although both combine intense fruitiness with a remarkably fresh sea taste. Glen Scotia is currently mothballed – a term which is applied to distilleries which are no longer producing whisky but are kept in working condition. Glen Scotia is due to go into production again in 1999, and Springbank distillery can be visited but by appointment only.

Speyside

The Speyside distilleries are the biggest grouping in Scotland, with over 40 working distilleries. They are often described as the most elegant and complex of the malts. At one extreme there are the light, malty

Glenfiddich Distillery.

ones like Glenlivet, Glen Grant and Glenfiddich. At the other, the rich and well-sherried ones like Glenfarclas and Macallan. All these distilleries can be visited. Between these two extremes there lies a vast spectrum of flavours and types. Longmorn's oily fruitiness has already been mentioned, but there are other exceptions. Knockando, for example, has a pronounced nutty character, as well as something reminiscent of good eau-de-vie or grappa, although the distillery itself cannot be visited. Other malts from this area include Tamnavulin, a light sweet whisky and Cardhu, which produces a round, sweet peaty spirit. They are all different, most are good and several are truly great. Tamnavulin is at present mothballed but the distillery can still be visited, as can Cardhu.

Islay

Seven working distilleries are left on the island, and all produce whiskies of merit. The four on the south coast – Ardbeg, Bowmore, Laphroaig and Lagavulin – all smoke the barley quite heavily. The Islay peat gives all the island whisky an iodine quality not found in the mainland whiskies. These malts have such pronounced flavours, particularly the medicinal overtones of Lagavulin, that many people find them too powerful.

Lagavulin Distillery.

Of the other three – Bruichladdich, Bunnahabhain and Caol Ila – the first two do not use nearly as much smoke in the production process, and so the smell of the sea comes through more, rather than the iodine. Caol Ila, on the other hand, is more like the ones from the south in style and taste, as it has a light well-rounded flavour with a peppery aftertaste. All the remaining distilleries on Islay, except Bruichladdich which is mothballed, are open to the public.

Island

The other five island malts are harder to categorise. Soft, malty Isle of Jura would not be out of place on the mainland. Talisker, a full-bodied malt from Skye, does have a slight whiff of iodine, but also a unique peppery flavour along with smoky flavours. Both distilleries are open to the public. Highland Park– produced on Orkney, despite its somewhat confusing name – is malty and fruity. However, it also has a good proportion of sherry flavour and smoke to it as well. Because the distillers also throw heather onto the peat during the drying process, the smoke has a woody overtone along with the more straightforward peat flavour. Highland Park can be visited but the other distillery on Orkney, Scapa, is currently mothballed.

Isle of Arran whisky, the youngest of the whisky distilleries, celebrated its whisky 'coming of age' in 1998, whilst Tobermory on Mull, is also becoming more readily available. Both of these single malts show little evidence of peatiness and are generally light in character.

The Distilleries

and some other places of interest

Map of Distilleries

and Other Sites

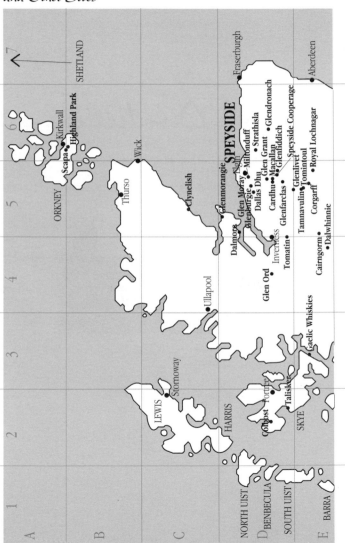

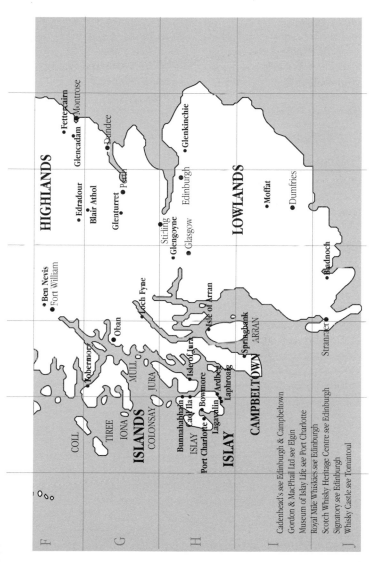

List of Distilleries

Ardbeg Distillery

On A846, 2.5 miles E of Port Ellen, Ardbeg, Islay (H3).

The distillery was founded in 1815 by the MacDougalls of Ardbeg, and the white-washed buildings are situated on the picturesque southern coast of Islay, near to Laphroaig and Lagavulin. Ardbeg has had a chequered

past, and was closed for many years, but in 1997 was bought over by Glenmorangie plc and recommissioned. The spirit produced here is made from the distillery's own private water source from Loch Uigeadail, and is made in unusual stills with their 'purifier', which contributes to the quality and fine balance of the whisky. Ardbeg is a peaty whisky, but gives way to the sweetness of the malt.

The visitor centre is housed in the distillery's original kiln and malt barn, which has displays of old artefacts from the distillery and features tales from the past. The shop has a wide range of Ardbeg malt whiskies and gifts. The tour charge is redeemable on any purchase over £15.00.

Open all year, Mon-Fri 10.00-16.00, Jun-Aug also Sat & Sun 10.00-17.00; last full tour 15.30; also by appt.

Guided tours. Gift shop. Old Kiln Coffee shop. WC. Limited disabled access. Maximum ten per group. Prebooking advisable for larger groups. Parking. £.

Tel: 01496 302244   Fax: 01496 302040

Ben Nevis Distillery

On A82, 2 miles N of Fort William, Lochy Bridge, Highland (F4).

Standing by Scotland's highest mountain, the Ben Nevis Distillery was founded in 1825 by Long John MacDonald from Keppoch, whose ancestors had fought at the Battle of Culloden in 1746. It was visited by Queen Victoria in 1848. Long John died in 1865, and Ben Nevis was taken over by his son. By 1885 it was producing over 150,000 gallons of malt whisky a year. Two years later the plant included an engineers' shop, cooperage, joinery shop and a saw mill, cart sheds, stables and stores, as well as an arable farm of 5000 acres. A pier was constructed at Loch Linnhe so that the whisky could be delivered using the distillery's own steamers. Ben Nevis was sold by the MacDonalds in 1955, and went through several decades of change and closure, only to be reopened in 1990 after being bought by the Nikka Whisky Distilling Company.

The distillery produces the Ben Nevis Single Highland Malt, which is a rich, substantial whisky with a full malty taste.

There is a 30-minute tour of the distillery and an exhibition and audio-visual presentation are also available in the vistor centre. A sample of 'The Dew of Ben Nevis' is included in the admission charge which is also redeemable in the shop as a discount on a 70cl bottle of malt whisky.

Open all year Mon-Fri 9.00-17.00; Easter and weekends, Sat 10.00-16.00; Jul & Aug 9.00-19.30; last tour leaves 30 mins before closing.

Guided tours. Audio-visual and explanatory displays. Giftshop. Tearoom. WC. Car and coach parking.

Tel: 01397 700200/702476   Fax: 01397 702768

Bladnoch Distillery

On A714, 9 miles S of Newton Stewart, Bladnoch, Dumfries & Galloway (J4).

The most southerly distillery in Scotland, Bladnoch was founded in 1817 by John and Thomas MacClelland, and uses water from the River Bladnoch. It passed to the Irish whiskey distillers, Dunvilles, but they sold it for a loss in 1936. The distillery closed two years later, but was recommissioned in 1956, only to be closed again in 1993, by which time it was owned by United Distillers, although it has since passed again into Irish hands.

The 10-Year-Old Single Malt Whisky has a fresh, delicate fruity flavour.

It has recently reopened, and a tour of the distillery, followed by a free sample of whisky, is available. There are woodland and river walks and picnic areas nearby.

Open late-Mar–early-Nov, Mon-Fri 9.00-17.00; Nov-Dec 11.00-15.30.

Guided tours. Explanatory displays. Gift shop. Picnic and BBQ area. River woodland walks. WC. Car and coach parking. £.

Tel: 01988 402605   Fax: 01988 402605

Blair Athol Distillery

On A924, 1 mile S of Pitlochry, Perthshire (G5).

Established in 1798 in the popular Perthshire town of Pitlochry, Blair Athol Distillery is one of the oldest working distilleries in Scotland. It is now owned by United Distillers and Vintners. Whisky produced here is used in Bell's Eight-Year-Old Extra Special, the biggest-selling blended whisky in the UK, and the water comes from the Allt Dour, the burn of the Otter.

The 12-Year-Old Malt has a fresh, peaty, nutty, spicy flavour.

A free dram is given after the tour, and the admission charge includes a discount voucher, which is redeemable in the well-stocked distillery shop towards the purchase of a 70cl bottle of malt whisky. Children under eight years are welcome but are not encouraged to take the tour.

Open Easter-Sep, Mon-Sat 9.00-17.00, Sun 12.00-17.00, last tour 16.00; Oct-Easter, Mon-Fri 9.00-17.00, last tour 15.30; Dec-Feb restricted opening hours – tel for appt.

Guided tours. Explanatory displays. Gift shop. Coffee shop. Banqueting suite available for private parties. WC. Car and coach parking – groups should book in advance. Group concessions. £.

Tel: 01796 482003   Fax: 01796 482001

Bowmore Distillery

Off A846, School Street, Bowmore, Islay (H2).

Bowmore (pronounced 'beau -more') Distillery is one of the oldest in Scotland, and was licensed in 1779. The distillery uses the traditional method of producing its own floor-malted barley. The water comes from the Laggan River. A fine malt whisky is produced here, relatively light for an Islay malt, peaty but with a balanced sweetness, and is available as Legend, 12-, 15-, 17-, 21-, 25-, 30-, and 40-Year-Old.

The distillery offers guided tours and a video presentation explaining the process of whisky making. The admission charge is redeemable in the shop, which stocks a full range of Bowmore Islay single malt Scotch whiskies. The tour includes a dram.

Across the entrance yard, a former warehouse, gifted to the local community, is now a swimming pool heated by waste energy from the distillery.

Open May-Sep, Mon-Fri: guided tours at 10.30, 11.30, 14.00 & 15.00, Sat 10.30, closed Sun; Oct-Apr, Mon-Fri 10.30 and 14.00.

Guided tours. Explanatory displays. Gift shop. Visitors receive a dram of whisky. Disabled access: walkways ramped for wheelchairs & WC. Car and coach parking. Group concessions. £. Booking advisable for groups.

Tel: 01496 810671   Fax: 01496 810757   Web: www.morrisonbowmore.co.uk

Bunnahabhain Distillery

Off A846, 3.5 miles N of Port Askaig, Bunnahabhain, Islay (H2).

Bunnahabhain is Gaelic for 'mouth of the river' and is pronounced 'Boon-na-ha-ven'. It is the most northerly of Islay's distilleries, in a peaceful and picturesque location on the Sound of Islay with views of Jura and to Mull. It was built between 1881 and 1883 by the Greenless Brothers, Islay farmers. The distillery was amalgamated with Glenrothes-Glenlivet to form the Highland Distillers Co Ltd, who still own both distilleries to this day. Bunnahabhain was extended in 1963 to cope with increased production.

The 12-Year-Old has a round, smooth flavour and is less peaty than some of the other Islay malts. Bunnahabhain is also the home of Black Bottle Blended Scotch Whisky, which is a rich mix of all seven malts produced on Islay.

Visitors are welcome and are given a guided tour of the distillery. Individuals and groups are welcome, and the tour includes a dram of the Bunnahabhain 12-Year-Old Islay Malt Scotch Whisky.

Open all year except closed Christmas and New Year, Mon-Fri 10.00-16.00 – distillery tours by appt only.

Guided tours by arrangement. Gift shop. WC. Car and coach parking. Accommodation available in cottages.

Tel: 01496 840646   Fax: 01496 840248

Caol Ila Distillery

Off A846, N of Port Askaig, Caol Ila (signposted), Islay (H2).

Caol Ila (pronounced 'Caal-eela') Distillery stands in a picturesque setting at the foot of a steep hill, with a small pier, overlooking the Sound of Islay and Paps of Jura, and local wildlife includes seals and otters. It was built in 1846 by Hector Henderson but then changed hands. By the 1880s the distillery was producing 147,000 gallons of whisky a year; it even had its own steam ship, 'The Pibroch', which transported the whisky to Glasgow. The distillery is now owned by United Distillers and Vintners.

The popularity of the whisky led to a major expansion in the 1970s, and most of the production is still used in famous brands such as Bell's, the best-selling blended Scotch Whisky in the UK. A 15-Year-Old Malt is also produced here, which can be sampled after the tour. It has a light, well-rounded, medium-peated flavour with a long dry peppery aftertaste.

A visit involves a personal tour, and the shop has a wide range of blended whiskies and well as the Caol Ila Malt Whisky. The adult admission includes a redeemable voucher towards the purchase of a 70cl bottle of malt whisky. Children under eight years of age are welcome but are not encouraged to take the tour.

Open all year, Mon-Fri by appt; at various times of the year the distillery is not in production although visitors are welcome and tours are provided.

Visitor centre. Guided tours by arrangement. Gift shop. WC. Car parking. & but includes redeemable voucher. Children under eight years are welcome but are not encouraged to take the tour.

Tel: 01496 840207   Fax: 01496 302763

Cardhu Distillery

On B9102, 17 miles NE of Grantown-on-Spey, Knockando, Moray (D5).

Cardhu, (pronounced 'Car-doo' and meaning 'black rock' in Gaelic) was licensed in 1824, but the origins of the distillery go back to the days of illicit whisky distilling, when crofters made their own spirit from barley and water. The distillery was founded by the Cumming family, who improved and expanded it over many years.

Cardhu is now an integral part of the Johnnie Walker company, itself part of United Distillers and Vintners. The whisky produced here is used in the Johnnie Walker blended whiskies, but a 12-Year-Old Malt Whisky, which has a round, sweet peaty flavour, is also produced. Cardhu uses water taken from springs on the Mannoch Hill and the Lyne Burn, and has six stills.

The visitor centre features an exhibition depicting the history of Cardhu and Johnnie Walker, and a tour includes a complimentary dram. The admission charge is redeemable in shop against the purchase of a 70cl bottle of Cardhu single malt.

Open Mar-Nov, Mon-Fri, 9.30-16.30; Jul-Sep also Sat 9.30-16.30, Sun 11.00-16.00; Dec-Feb, Mon-Fri 10.00-16.00; closed Christmas and New Year.

Guided tours. Explanatory displays. Gift shop. Picnic area. Disabled access. Car and coach parking. Large parties by appt only.

Tel: 01340 872555/810204   Fax: 01340 872556

Clynelish Distillery

On A9, 1 mile NW of Brora, Clynelish, Sutherland (C5).

Clynelish (pronounced 'Clyn-leesh') Distillery was built in 1819 by the Marquis of Stafford, later to become Duke of Sutherland, whose castle at Dunrobin is open to the public. The distillery used locally grown grain and was fired by coal from a nearby mine, and the water comes from the Clynemilton Burn. The distillery was extended in 1896 by the Leith Whisky blenders, Ainslie and Co. In 1967 the new distillery was built near the original building to meet the increased demand for whisky. Clynelish is available as a 14-Year-Old Single Malt, a full-bodied whisky with slight fruity overtones, and is a key component of Johnnie Walker's 'Gold Label' blend. The distillery is now owned by United Distillers and Vintners.

A tour of the distillery is available, and the shop in the visitor centre stocks the Clynelish Malt Whisky and the exclusive Johnnie Walker 'Gold Label' 18-Year-Old Blend. Children under eight years of age are welcome but are not encouraged to take the tour. The admission charge includes a voucher redeemable at the distillery towards the purchase of a 70cl bottle of malt whisky.

Open Mar-Oct, Mon-Fri 9.30-16.00; Nov-Feb Mon-Thu 9.30-16.30; last tour 16.00; or by appt.

Guided tours. Gift shop. Picnic area. Garden. WC. Disabled access. Car and coach parking. £.

Tel: 01408 623014/623000   Fax: 01408 623004

Dallas Dhu Distillery

Off A940, 1 mile S of Forres, Dallas Dhu, Moray (D5).

A well-preserved Victorian distillery, Dallas Dhu (pronounced 'Dallas Doo') is no longer in production but was built in 1898 to supply malt whisky for Wright and Greig's 'Roderick Dhu' blend. The water for the distillery came from the Altyre Burn, and the bulk of its output was taken to Glasgow for blending, although Dallas Dhu was (and is) also available as a single malt, a rich, smooth flavoured whisky. The distillery, and the industry more generally, fared badly from 1890, and it changed hands several times. Although it did well in the 1950s and 1960s, it closed in 1983. The distillery was taken into the care of the State, and is now managed by Historic Scotland.

Access is available to most areas of the distillery, and there is an audio-visual presentation which also includes a dram.

Open all year: Apr-Sep Mon-Sat 9.30-6.30, Sun 2-6.30; Oct-Mar Mon-Sat 9.30-4.30, Sun 2-4.30; closed Thu PM and Fri in winter; closed 25/26 Dec & 1-3 Jan.

Visitor centre. Guided tours. Explanatory displays. Audio-visual presentation. Gift shop. Picnic area. WC. Limited disabled access. Car and coach parking. Group concessions. £.

Tel: 01309 676548

Dalmore Distillery

On B817, 1 mile SE of Alness, Dalmore, Ross and Cromarty (D5).

Located in a scenic position overlooking the Black Isle and Cromarty Firth, the distillery was founded in 1839 by Alexander Matheson, a merchant. It was acquired by the Mackenzie family in 1886, then Whyte and Mackay, who are now owned by American Brands. It was used as a factory to manufacture mines in World War I and was burned down, but rebuilt in 1922. The distillery has had eight stills since 1966, and uses water from the River Alness. It produces the Dalmore Single Highland Malt, which is a fresh, rich well-balanced whisky.

Tours of the distillery are available by appointment only.

Open by appt only. Groups limited to ten at most.

Tel: 01349 882362   Fax: 01349 883655

Dalwhinnie Distillery

Off A9, Dalwhinnie, Highland (E4).

Dalwhinnie, which in Gaelic means 'the meeting place', was a resting point for Highland drovers on their way to cattle markets at Crieff and Falkirk. The distillery is the highest in Scotland, at over 1000 feet. It was opened in 1898, and now is owned by United Distillers and Vintners. The water for the distillery comes from Allt an t'Sluie, a spring which is a source of the Spey river. A single

malt 'Gentle Spirit', is produced here, a light whisky with a honey-sweet flavour.

Tour guides explain the distilling process. The exhibition features James Buchan, a licensee of the distillery, famed for his 'Buchanan' and 'Black and White' blends; the history and geography of the area; and the Classic Malts. The shop in the visitor centre has an extensive range of single malt whiskies, and the admission includes a discount voucher redeemable in the distillery shop towards a purchase of a 70cl bottle of malt whisky. Children under eight years of age are welcome but are not admitted to the production areas.

Open Mar-Dec, Mon-Fri 9.30-16.30; Jun-Oct also Sat 9.30-16.30; Jul & Aug also Sun 2.30-16.30; Jan & Feb by appt as restricted hours may operate due to extreme weather conditions; closed Christmas & New Year period.

Guided tours. Visitor centre with explanatory displays. Gift shop. WC. Car and coach parking. Group concessions. &. Parties of more than 12 are asked to make a reservation in advance.

Tel: 01528 522208   Fax: 01528 522296

Edradour Distillery

On A924, 2.5 miles E of Pitlochry, Edradour (signposted), Perthshire (F5).

Pronounced 'Eddra-dower' and named after a local burn, Edradour was founded in 1825 by a group of local farmers, and is Scotland's smallest distillery and one of the most picturesque. It has remained virtually unchanged since Victorian times, and consists of solid white-washed buildings with grey-slate roofs. The distillery is owned by Campbell Distillers Ltd. Water comes from soft spring water on Moulin Moor, and the Edradour 10-Year-Old Single Malt has a light, nutty flavour.

A dram of whisky is offered during an audio-visual show in the visitor centre in the malt barn.

Open Mar-Oct, Mon-Sat 9.30-17.00, Sun 12.00-17.00; Nov-Feb, Mon-Sat 10.00-16.00 shop only; closed Christmas & New Year

Guided tours and audio-visual presentation. Explanatory displays. Gift shop. WC. Car and coach parking. Groups over 14 by appt only.

Tel: 01796 472095   Fax: 01796 472002

Fettercairn Distillery

Off A90, Distillery Road, 0.5 miles W of Fettercairn, Kincardine & Deeside (F6).

Believed to be one of the oldest 'legal' distilleries in Scotland, Fettercairn was licensed in 1824 and was visited by Queen Victoria. It is now owned by JBB (Greater Europe) Plc. The water comes from springs in the Grampian Mountains, and it produces the Old Fettercairn Single Malt Scotch Whisky, a light and sweet malt.

   The distillery visitor centre offers tours describing the process of whisky making, and there is an audio-visual presentation, charting the Fettercairn story and history of the Mearns. A visit includes a free dram of Old Fettercairn, and the tour is free of charge.

Open May-Sep 10.00-16.30; last tour 16.00.

Visitor centre. Guided tours. Explanatory displays. Gift shop. WC. Car and coach parking. Groups by appt only.

Tel: 01561 340205/244   Fax: 01561 340447

Glen Grant Distillery

On A941, 3.5 miles N of Aberlour, Rothes, Moray (D5).

Located in a wooded, sheltered glen on the outskirts of the Speyside village of Rothes, the distillery was founded in 1840 by two brothers, James and John Grant. Major John Grant, their successor, modernised the plant, introducing refrigerated coolers in 1877, and from 1886 the buildings were lit by electricity. The water comes from the Caperdonich Well, and the distillery has coal-fired stills.

Glen Grant has been owned by Seagrams since 1977, and production expanded with the addition of further stills in 1973 and 1977. The whisky produced here has a distinctive flavour: light in colour, bright and crisp, slightly dry with a fruity finish, and is hugely popular in Italy.

Tours of the distillery are available, and feature an audio-visual presentation and access to a restored Victorian garden, created by Major James Grant. Admission price includes a voucher redeemable against 70cl bottle of whisky, distillery tour and access to garden. Children under the age of eight years are not admitted to production areas.

Open Mar-May & Oct, Mon-Sat 10.00-16.00, Sun 11.30-16.00; Jun-Sep, Mon-Sat 10.00-17.00, Sun 11.30-17.00.

Free to under-18s. Gift shop. WC. Disabled limited access & WC. Car parking. £.

Tel: 01542 783318   Fax: 01542 783304

Glen Moray Distillery

Off A96, W of Elgin, Moray (D5).

Situated on the banks of the River Lossie close to the ancient cathedral city and royal burgh of Elgin, the Glen Moray distillery was developed from a brewery in 1897. The original brewery buildings date from 1815. It has been in almost con-tinuous production and was among only a handful of selected distilleries that were allowed to continue production during World War II in order to assist the national debt. It was acquired by MacDonald and Muir in 1920, and in 1958 it was refurbished with production capacity doubled from two to four stills.

Glen Moray Distillery has recently relaunched its fine range of single malts, which are smooth, dry and light Speyside whiskies. They have been mellowed for a final period in white-wine barrels.

Open all year: Mon-Fri 9.00-17.00; tours at 9.30, 10.30, 11.30, 14.00, 15.00 and 16.00; closed for two weeks over Christmas and New Year.

Tel: 01343 542577   Fax: 01343 546195

Email: pauline@glenmoray.com   Web: www.glenmoray.com

Glen Ord Distillery

Off A832, 15 miles W of Inverness, Muir of Ord, Highland (D4).

The last survivor of nine distilleries which once operated around Glen Ord, the distillery was licensed in 1838. It was acquired by John Dewar in 1923, and extended from two to six stills in 1966. Glen Ord is owned by

United Distillers and Vintners, and licensed to them. The water for the distillery comes from the 'White Burn' flowing from Loch nan Eun and Loch nam Bonnach, and the 12-Year-Old Malt has a full-bodied, slightly dry flavour.

The tour and exhibition show the history of the Black Isle and the main processes of distilling. A free dram is part of the adult admission charge, which also includes a discount voucher redeemable in the distillery shop towards the purchase of a 70cl bottle of malt whisky.

Open all year: Mon-Fri 9.30-17.00; Jul & Aug also Sat 9.30-17.00 & Sun 12.30-17.00; closed Christmas and New Year.

Visitor centre. Guided tours. Explanatory displays. Gift shop. Picnic area. WC. Disabled access. Car and coach parking. Group concessions. £.

Tel: 01463 872004   Fax: 01463 872008   Web: www.glenord.com

Glenburgie Distillery

Off A96, 3.5 miles E of Forres, Glenburgie, Moray (D5).

Set in a very attractive landscaped location, Glenburgie Distillery, first established in 1810, was replaced towards the end of the 19th century by William Paul, and uses water from local springs. The distillery was closed between 1927 and 1935, but was reopened and is now run by Allied Distillers. Output from the distillery is used in Ballantine's blended whisky, and the Glenburgie 8-Year-Old Single Malt which is a light, slightly dry whisky.

Tours of the distillery are available but only by previous arrangement.

By appt only.

Tel: 01343 850258   Fax: 01343 850480

Glencadam Distillery

Off A935, 0.5 miles E of Brechin, Angus (F6).

Believed to have been established in 1825, the distillery was purchased by Hiram Walker in 1954, but is now operated by Allied Distillers. The water comes from springs in the Unthank Hills, and there are two stills. The Glencadam 1974 Single Malt has a full-bodied, smoky flavour.

Tours of the distillery are by appointment only.

Open Sep-Jun, Mon-Thu 14.00-16.00; maximum ten people in parties; all visits by appt only.

Tel: 01356 622217   Fax: 01356 624926

Glenfiddich Distillery

On A941, just N of Dufftown, Moray (D5).

Set close to the impressive and historic Balvenie Castle, the distillery was founded in 1887 by William Grant of Glenfiddich, and has remained in the Grant family ever since. The distillery uses water from the Robbie Dhu springs, and has 28 stills. This was the first distillery to open a visitor centre, and has over 100,000 visitors a year. Glenfiddich is the only Highland single malt Scotch whisky to be distilled, matured and bottled at its own plant. The 18-Year-Old Ancient Reserve has a rounded, mellow flavour.

Tours cover the whisky-making process at its various stages, and a free dram is included. There is an audio-visual presentation about the history and manufacture of whisky and the heritage of the Highlands – plus a Scotch whisky display.

Open all year weekdays 9.30-16.30 excluding Christmas and New Year holidays. In addition open Easter-mid-Oct, Sat 9.30-16.30, Sun 12.00-16.30. Parties of more than twelve people welcome but please contact distillery.

Visitor centre. Guided tours. Explanatory displays. Gift shop. Picnic area. WC. Disabled access. Coach and car parking.

Tel: 01340 820373   Fax: 01340 820805

Web: www.glenfiddich.com

Glengoyne Distillery

On A81, 2 miles S of Killearn, Dumgoyne, Stirlingshire (H4).

Located in the Campsie Fells, Glengoyne Distillery was first licensed in 1833, and is Scotland's most southerly Highland distillery. The distillery was purchased by Lang Brothers in 1876, and is still owned by the same company. It draws water from a 50-foot waterfall in the Glengoyne Burn, to the north of the 'Highland Line', and produces Scotland's only unpeated whisky. Naturally malted barley is used here, and the whisky produced is smooth and refined, with a light, fresh, delicate nose.

  The distillery offers tours, and there is a shop and Heritage Room, which houses a cooperage display, and old artefacts. Admission includes a free dram.

Open all year: Mon-Sat 10.00-16.00, Sun 12.00-16.00; closed 25 Dec & 1 Jan.

Guided tours. Explanatory displays. Gift shop. Scenic waterfall walk. WC. Disabled access, Car and coach parking. &. Evening functions can be booked, and parties of ten or more should make prior bookings.

Tel: 01360 550254   Fax: 01360 550094   Web: www.glengoyne.com

Glenkinchie Distillery

On A6093, 2.5 miles S of Pencaitland, East Lothian (H6).

Set in a small glen in East Lothian, Glenkinchie is the only remaining malt whisky distillery close to Edinburgh. It was founded in 1837 by the brothers John and George Rate, who were local farmers, although it was closed between 1853 and 1880. Much of the distillery dates from Victorian times as the plant was rebuilt and expanded in 1890. It is now owned by United Distillers and Vintners.

The water comes from the Lammermuir Hills, and the Glenkinchie 10-Year-Old Single Malt Whisky, 'The Edinburgh Malt', has a light body and a smooth dry aftertaste with a soft, aromatic nose.

Visitors can see all aspects of the traditional distilling craft on a tour of the distillery. Features a unique exhibition of malt whisky production, and includes a scale model of a malt whisky distillery made for the British Empire Exhibition of 1924. The admission charge is redeemable in the shop.

Open all year: Jun-Oct Mon-Sat 9.30-17.00, Sun 12.00-17.00; Oct-Apr, Mon-Fri 9.30-17.00; last tour 16.00.

Guided tours. Visitor centre with explanatory displays. Gift shop. Picnic area. WC. Disabled access. Car and coach parking. Group concessions. £. Groups by appt only.

Tel: 01875 342004   Fax: 01875 342007

Glenlivet Distillery

Off B9008, 10 miles N of Tomintoul, Glenlivet, Moray (E5).

Established in the face of opposition from illicit whisky makers and smugglers, Glenlivet Distillery was founded by George Smith, a tenant of the Duke of Gordon, in 1824 at Upper Drummin Farm. The old distillery was destroyed by fire, and the plant was moved to Minore in 1858. It uses water from Josie's Well. The Glenlivet was amalgamated with J & J Grant in 1953, and has been owned by Seagrams since 1977. The Glenlivet 12-Year-Old Single Malt Scotch Whisky is a light, smooth whisky with a delicately sweet flavour, and there is also an 18-Year-Old.

The tour of the distillery includes whisky production facilities and bonded warehouses, and features an audio-visual programme and interactive exhibition. The admission includes a voucher redeemable against the purchase of a 70cl bottle of whisky in the distillery shop, entry to exhibition, guided tour of distillery and free dram of whisky.

Open Mar-Oct, Mon-Sat 10.00-16.00, Sun 12.30 16.00; Jul & Aug closes 18.00. Children under age of eight are not admitted to production areas.

Free to under-18s. Visitor centre with audio-visual programme and exhibition. Gift shop. Disabled access to visitor centre. Parking. £ (includes voucher for shop). Under 18s admitted free.

Tel: 01542 783220   Fax: 01542 783218

Glenmorangie Distillery

On A9, 1 mile N of Tain, Glenmorangie, Ross & Cromarty (D5).

Glenmorangie (which is pronounced 'Glen -MORangie' which means 'the glen of tranquillity' in Gaelic) was converted from a brewery and licensed in 1843. The distillery has been owned by Macdonald and Muir since 1918. The water comes from the Tarlogie Springs, and the Glenmorangie 10-Year-Old Single Malt is an extremely popular whisky: medium-bodied with a lightly, sweet flavour.

  The visitor centre is housed in the original still-house, and features a 130-year-old working steam engine, and stories and artefacts from the distillery's past. Visitors can tour the distillery, and the admission charge is redeemable.

Open all year: shop Mon-Fri 9.00-17.00, Sat 10.00-16.00, Sun 12.00-16.00; tours available from 10.30; last tour 15.30; prebooking advisable: maximum fifteen per group.

Guided tour. Explanatory displays. Gift shop. WC. Car and coach parking. Disabled facilities. £.

Tel: 01862 892477   Fax: 01862 893862

Email: Visitors@Glenmorangieplc.Co.Uk   Web: www.glenmorangie.com

Glenturret Distillery

Off A85, 1 mile W of Crieff, Hosh, Perthshire (G5).

In a picturesque location near the town of Crieff – and formerly called Hosh – Glenturret Distillery dates from 1775 and is the oldest in Scotland. It was renamed Glenturret in 1875, and is one of Scotland's smallest distilleries. It was closed from 1923 to 1959, but has since been established as one of the most popular malts: strong, smooth and mellow. It uses the water of the Turret Burn with the 'pot still' process, a tradition unchanged since it began in the 18th century. The shop sells a range of award-winning Glenturret whiskies.

A tour of the distillery includes a free tasting and an audio-visual presentation, called 'Water of Life', in the visitor centre as well as the 'Spirit of the Glen' exhibition. The shop sells a range of Glenturret whiskies.

Open Feb-Dec, Mon-Sat 9.30-18.00, Sun 12.00-18.00 (last tour 16.30); Jan Mon-Fri 11.30-16.00; (last tour 14.30).

Guided tours. Audio-visual presentation and exhibition. Gift shop. Smuggler's Restaurant and bar. WC. Disabled access and WC. Car and coach parking. £.

Tel: 01764 656565   Fax: 01764 654366

Email: Glenturret@HighlandDistillers.co.uk   Web: www.glenturret.com

Highland Park Distillers

On A961, S of Kirkwall, Orkney (B6).

The most northerly whisky distillery in the world, Highland Park is located on a hillside with fine views over Scapa Flow. It stands on the site of an illicit still, and was founded in 1798, but had passed to the Grant family by 1900. It was acquired by Highland Distillers Co in 1935, and has four stills. Water comes from springs below the distillery, and it still uses traditional floor maltings. The Highland Park 12-Year-Old has a smooth, smoky flavour, and 18- and 25-Year Olds are also available.

   Tours of the distillery are available and there is a visitor centre.

Open Mar-Jun, Mon-Fri: tours every 30 mins from 10.00-16.00; Jul & Aug: also open wknds 12.00-16.00; Sep & Oct: Mon-Fri tours every 30 mins 10.00-16.00; Nov-Dec: tours at 14.00 & 15.30; Jan & Feb tours by appt only; closed Christmas and New Year.

Guided tours. Audio-visual and explanatory displays. Gift shop. WC. Disabled access. Car and coach parking. Group concessions. £.

Tel: 01856 874619   Fax: 01856 876091

Isle of Arran Distillery

Off A841, 14 miles N of Brodick, Lochranza, Arran (H3).

Set in a scenic location at Lochranza, Isle of Arran Distillery is the newest single malt whisky distillery in Scotland, having only been in production since 1995 – the first legal distillery on Arran for 150 years. The distillery uses water from Eason Biorach, a mountain burn; has traditional washbacks; specially commissioned stills; and has its own warehousing on site. The whisky is still quite young but has a well-rounded malty flavour.

View of Arran.

The visitor centre features interactive displays and a short film illustrating whisky production on Arran over the last 150 years; and a tour concludes with a free dram. An audio-visual room is located in the mock 18th-century crofter's inn.

Open daily all year 10.00-17.00; closed Christmas and New Year; for group booking contact the distillery; restaurant open 11.00-22.00; closed Wed evening; winter opening times vary.

Visitor centre. Guided tours. Audio-visual programme and explanatory displays. Gift shop. Restaurant. Picnic area. Garden. WC. Disabled access. Induction loop for audio-visual programme. Car and coach parking. ££. Coach parties welcome but should tel in advance. Private functions and conference facilities.

Tel: 01770 830264   Fax: 01770 830364

Email: arran.distillers@btinternet.com   Web: www.arranwhisky.com

Isle of Jura Distillery

On A846, Craighouse, Jura (H3).

On the wild and picturesque island of Jura, the original distillery was built in 1810, close to where illegal distilling had occurred for 300 years. The distillery was built by the Campbells and could produce 720 gallons of whisky a week. It was leased to James Ferguson in 1875, and completely rebuilt in 1884. When the lease expired, the Campbells tried to increase the rent – but Ferguson dismantled the distillery and sold the machinery. The present distillery was built in 1963, extended in 1971, and belongs to JBB (Greater Europe) Plc. The water comes from Loch a' Bhaile Mhargaidh – 'Market Loch'. The 10-Year-Old Single Malt is a light, slightly smoky, sweet-flavoured whisky.

Open by appointment only.

Open by appt.

Guided tours. Car parking.

Tel: 01496 820240   Fax: 01496 820344

Craighouse, Jura.

Lagavulin Distillery

On A846, 2 miles E of Port Ellen, Lagavulin, Islay (H2).

Near the ruins of Dunyvaig Castle, ancient stronghold of the Lords of the Isles, Lagavulin (pronounced 'Lagga-voolin') Distillery, was established in 1816 by John Johnson. Production from here goes to the White Horse blend. The water used is from the Solum Lochs. The distillery is now owned by United Distillers and Vintners, and also produces a distinctive

malt whisky, which is very peaty and full bodied with a hint of ozone.

Tours and tastings can be taken by appointment, and the adult charge includes a discount voucher redeemable at the distillery against a 70cl bottle of malt whisky. Tours are by appointment only; please telephone in advance.

Open Apr-Oct, Mon-Fri. Tours at 10.00, 11.30 & 14.30 and are by appt only.

Guided tours. Explanatory displays. Gift shop. WC. Car and coach parking. £. Children under the age of eight are welcome but are not encouraged to take the tour.

Tel: 01496 302400 Fax: 01496 302733

Laphroaig Distillery

Off A846, 1 mile E of Port Ellen, Laphroaig, Islay (H2).

Located in a scenic bay with otters and swans, the original distillery at Laphroaig (pronounced 'La-froyg' and meaning 'the beautiful hollow by the broad bay') was founded by Donald and Alex Johnston in 1815 and is housed in white-washed buildings. It remained with the same family until 1954 and is now operated by Allied Distillers. The distillery uses water from the Kilbride Dam, and production was expanded with the addition of new stills in 1923, 1969 and 1974. The distillery still uses its own floor maltings: the malted barley is dried over a peat fire.

The whisky produced here is probably the most unusual of all malts, with quite a unique flavour which is said to derive from the peat. Its strong peaty flavour has iodine and medicinal overtones, and is available as a 10-Year-Old and a 15-Year-Old, and – for the collector – a 30-Year-Old.

Tours of the distillery are available by appointment, and there is a shop.

Open all year, Mon-Thu: tours 10.30 & 14.00 by appt only; closed Jul & first two weeks in Aug.

Guided tours. Gift shop. WC. Disabled access. Car and coach parking.

Tel: 01496 302418   Fax: 01496 302496

Email: 106523.565@compuserve.com   Web: www.laphroaig.com

Macallan Distillery

Off B9102, 1 mile NE of Aberlour, Easter Elchies, Moray (D5).

Standing in a beautiful 400-acre estate high above the River Spey, the Macallan Distillery was officially licensed in 1824. The restored fortified house of Easter Elchies lies at the heart of the site. Estate-grown barley, the smallest stills on Speyside and exclusive maturation in sherry oak casks from Spain combine to create the rich, sherried spice and dried fruit flavour of the Macallan.

The distillery can be visited, but by appointment only.

By appt only.

Gift shop. Audio-visual presentation.

Tel: 01340 871471 Fax: 01340 871212

Web: www.themacallan-themalt.com

Miltonduff Distillery

Off B9010, 2 miles SW of Elgin, Miltonduff, Moray (D5).

Standing in a pleasant location not far from the historic town of Elgin, the distillery was founded in 1824 and is quite near the restored Abbey of Pluscarden. It was owned by Hiram Walker from 1936, but is now operated by Allied Distillers Ltd. There are six 'pot' stills, and water comes from a spring and borehole, while cooling water comes from the Black Burn. This burn is said to have been blessed by one of the abbots of Pluscarden, and thereafter the drink distilled from the burn was called *aqua vitae* or the water of life (*uisge beatha* in Gaelic). The 12-Year-Old Miltonduff Glenlivet Pure Single Malt is produced here, and is a fragrant, medium-bodied and lightly-peated malt.

The distillery offers tours by appointment and there is a reception centre.

Open Sep-Jun – tours available by appt only.

Tel: 01343 554121   Fax: 01343 548802

Oban Distillery

Off A816 or A85, Stafford Street, Oban, Argyll (G3).

In the holiday town of Oban, the distillery was established in 1794 by the Stevenson family, who were also involved in the development of the town. It was rebuilt in 1883 by Walter Higgin, and is now part of United Distillers and Vintners. The water comes from Loch Gleann A' Bhearraidh, and the malt produced here is mildly peated in flavour with a hint of the sea.

There are guided tours of the distillery and in the visitor centre there is an exhibition and audio-visual programme, which charts the history of Oban. The admission charge is redeemable towards the purchase of a 70cl bottle of malt whisky in the well-stocked shop. Children under eight years of age are welcome but are not permitted to tour the distillery.

Open all year, Mon-Fri 9.30-17.00; Jul-Sep, Mon-Fri 9.30-20.30; open Sat Easter-Oct 9.30-17.00; last tour leaves one hour before closing; Dec-Feb restricted hours; closed Christmas and New year period; booking advisable in winter months or when travelling any distance. Groups by appt only.

Guided tours. Exhibition. Gift shop. WC. Disabled access. Guide dogs not permitted. Parking nearby. £.

Tel: 01631 572004   Fax: 01631 572011

Email: Carol.J.Smith@guinness.com

Royal Lochnagar Distillery

Off B976, 5.5 miles W of Ballater, Crathie, Kincardine &
Deeside (E5).

About one mile from the royal family's castle at Balmoral, Royal Lochnagar was established in 1845 by John Begg, when it was known as New Lochnagar, as there was an older distillery nearby (which closed in 1860). Lochnagar became 'Royal' after a visit by Queen Victoria and Prince Albert in 1848. The distillery was rebuilt in 1906, then acquired by John Dewar and Sons in 1916. It is now part of United Distillers and Vintners, and the water comes from springs in the foothills of Lochnagar, a mountain which rises to

3789 feet. The distillery produces the Royal Lochnagar Single Highland Malt Scotch Whisky which has a medium-bodied taste with creamy, sweet overtones.

In the visitor centre, converted from the old distillery farm steading, there is a whisky shop and exhibition area.

Open all year: Easter-Oct, Mon-Sat 10.00-17.00, Sun 12.00-16.00; Nov-
Mar, Mon-Fri 10.00-17.00; closed Christmas and New Year. Children
under eight years of age are welcome but are not encouraged to take the
tour.

Guided tours. Explanatory displays. Whisky shop. WC. Parking nearby. £.

Tel: 01339 742273   Fax: 01339 742702

Scapa Distillery

On A964, 2 miles SW of Kirkwall, Scapa, Orkney (A6).

In a picturesque setting overlooking Scapa Flow, the Scapa distillery was established in 1885 by Macfarlane and Townsend. It was acquired by Hiram Walker in 1954, and is now operated by Allied Distillers Ltd, but was mothballed in 1994. It uses water from the Lingro Burn and nearby springs, and has two stills. The whisky produced here is used in Ballantine's blended Scotch Whisky, but there is also the Scapa Single Highland Malt, which is a clean, medium-bodied, firm whisky.

Tours can be made of the distillery by arrangement only.

Tours by appt only.

Tel: 01856 872071   Fax: 01856 876585

Springbank Distillery

Off A83, Campbeltown, Longrow, Kintyre (I3).

In the seaside town of Campbeltown in Kintyre, Springbank Distillery was founded in 1828, and is owned by the Mitchell family: J & A Mitchell and Company from 1897. The family had previously been involved in illicit whisky distilling – the great-great-grandfather of the present distiller had his still here – and this is the oldest distillery to be owned by the same family. From 1828 the distillery was licensed to the Reid family, before the Mitchells resumed direct management from 1837.

Campbeltown was once the centre for whisky distilling, with 30 legal distilleries, but Springbank is the only one currently operating – Glen Scotia is 'mothballed' although it is due to work for a period in 1999. Springbank has three stills, although only a proportion of the whisky is distilled three times, and uses water from Crosshill Loch. Springbank is unusual in that the whole process is undertaken on the same site: from floor maltings to bottling. The 21-Year-Old is a medium-bodied, slightly salty flavoured whisky.

Tours are available in the summer but are strictly by appointment only.

Distillery tours in summer strictly by appt.

Tel: 01586 552085   Fax: 01586 553215

Strathisla Distillery

Off A96, 0.5 miles N of Keith, Seafield Avenue, Moray (D6).

Strathisla (pronounced 'Strath-eye-la') Distillery, founded in 1786 as the Milton Distillery and said to be the oldest operating distillery in the Highlands, was converted to a flour mill in 1838. It was then reconverted to a distillery, before being damaged first by fire in 1876 and then by an explosion three years later. Produc-

tion was increased from two stills to four in 1965, and the distillery is the home of Chivas Regal, which is a subsidiary of Seagrams. As well as producing Chivas Regal – a rich and full malt whisky with a mellow finish – it also makes the Strathisla Single Malt Scotch Whisky in copper 'pot' stills with water from the Broomhill Spring.

A visit to the distillery features a self-guided tour of the distillery and includes a free dram, coffee and shortbread, guide book and whisky nosing, as well as a voucher redeemable against the purchase of a 70cl bottle of whisky. Children under the age of eight are not admitted to production areas

Open Feb-March, Mon-Fri 9.30-16.00; Mar-Nov, Mon-Sat 9.30-16.00, Sun 12.30-16.00.

Under-18s free. Reception centre with video presentation. Self-guided tours with coffee and shortbread (and sample whisky). Gift shop. Handbook. ££ (includes shop voucher). Under 18s free.

Tel: 01542 783044   Fax: 01542 783039

Talisker Distillery

On B8009, 6 miles W of Sligachan, Carbost, Skye (D2).

Beneath the impressive saw-toothed Cuillin mountains of Skye, the present distillery was founded in 1830 by Hugh and Kenneth MacAskill in a scenic location on the banks of Loch Harport. It was rebuilt in the 1890s, extended in 1900, but the still house was destroyed by fire in 1960, and the plant was rebuilt. It is now owned by United Distillers and Vintners, and has five stills and uses water from a burn on Cnoc nan Speireag: the malts produced here are full-bodied and peaty, with smoky flavours.

The distillery offers tours, but larger parties should book in advance: the approach road is not suitable for coaches. Adult admission includes a discount voucher redeemable in the well-stocked distillery shop towards the purchase of a 70cl bottle of malt whisky. Children under eight years of age are welcome but will not be admitted into the production area.

Open Apr-Jun & Oct, Mon-Fri 9.00-16.30; Jul-Sep, Mon-Sat 9.00-16.30; Nov-Mar, Mon-Fri 14.00-16.30; last tour at 14.00.

Guided tours. Explanatory displays. Gift shop. Picnic area. WC. Limited disabled access. Car parking. £.

Tel: 01478 640314   Fax: 01478 640401

Tamnavulin Distillery

On B9008, 4.5 miles NE of Tomintoul, Tomnavoulin, Moray (E5).

Tamnavulin (pronounced 'Tamna-VOO-lin') Distillery was founded in 1965-6 and is now owned by JBB (Greater Europe) Plc. It uses water from underground springs at Easterton, and produces light whiskies with sweet, floral overtones. The distillery is presently mothballed.

Tours of the distillery can be made. There is a coffee and gift shop.

Open Apr-Oct, Mon-Sat 9.30-16.30; Oct, Mon-Fri 9.30-16.30; Jul & Aug, also Sun 12.30-16.30.

Gift shop. Coffee shop. Audio-visual presentation. Limited disabled access. Parking.

Tel: 01807 590442   Fax: 01807 590342

Tobermory Distillery

Off A848, Tobermory, Mull (G3).

Located in the pleasant town of Tobermory, with its painted houses, on the scenic island of Mull, the distillery was established by John Sinclair, a local merchant, in 1798. It was acquired by John Hopkins and Son, who owned it until 1916, but closed between 1930 and 1972, and from 1989 to 1993 when it was purchased by Burn Stewart Distillers and reopened. It has four stills, uses unpeated, malted barley, and water from a private loch near Mishnish. The distillery produces the Tobermory Single Malt Scotch Whisky, which is a fresh, smooth and medium-dry malt.

The distillery offers tours and there is a visitor centre and shop.

Open Easter-Oct, Mon-Fri 10.00-17.00. Other times by appt.

Guided tours. Explanatory displays. Gift shop (entrance fee discounted on certain goods). Limited disabled access. Car and coach parking. &.

Tel: 01688 302645   Fax: 01688 302643

Tobermory, Mull.

Tomatin Distillery

Off A9, 15 miles S of Inverness, Tomatin, Highland (D4).

Tomatin was founded in 1897 by the Tomatin Spey District Distillery Co, then extended to four stills in 1956, six in 1958, ten in 1961, 11 in 1964, and finally 23 in 1974. It uses water from a local burn, the Allt-na-Frithe: the malt is light to medium-bodied, with clean, sweet and slightly gingery flavours.

There are tours of the distillery, and a free dram for visitors. The visitor centre features a fully stocked shop and an audio-visual presentation about the process and production of whisky.

Open all year, Mon-Fri 9.00-17.00; May-Oct also Sat 9.00-13.00; advance notice required in Dec & Jan.

Guided tours. Explanatory displays and video. Gift shop. WC. Disabled access. Car and coach parking.

Tel: 01808 511444   Fax: 01808 511373   Email: info@tomatin.co.uk

Tomintoul Distillery

On B9136, 3.5 miles N of Tomintoul, Moray (E5).

Tomintoul (pronounced 'Tom-in-towel') Distillery was founded in 1964-5, and was built by Tomintoul Distillery Ltd, but in 1990 was sold to American Brands Inc and is part of JBB (Greater Europe) Plc. There are four stills and the distillery uses water from the Ballantruan Spring. Tomintoul produces light, smooth and slightly sweetish malt whisky.

The distillery can be visited, but by appointment only.

By appt only. Group bookings limited to 10.

Tel: 01807 590274 Fax: 01807 590342

Other Places of Interest

Cadenhead's Whisky Shop

172 Canongate, Edinburgh EH8 8BN.

Independent whisky bottler. There are other branches at 3 Russell Street, Covent Garden, in London: tel: 0171 379 46404; fax: 0171 379 4600 and Reform Square,

Campbeltown, Argyll: tel: 01586 551710; fax: 01586 551110. Mail order service.

Open Mon-Sat, 10.30-17.30.

Tel: 0131 556 5864   Fax: 0131 556 2527

Cairngorm Whisky Centre

On B970, S of Aviemore, Inverdruie, Highland.

The whisky tasting room has whiskies from over 90 distilleries. Experts on hand for all aspects of Scotch whisky. The shop contains many old and rare whiskies, as well as miniatures, books, maps and Scottish fare.

Open daily, except Christmas and New Year, Mon-Sat 9.30-17.30 (later

opening in summer), Sun 12.30-16.30.

Explanatory displays. Gift shop. Tearoom. WC. Disabled access. Car parking. ££ for whisky tastings.

Tel: 01479 810574   Fax: 01479 810574

Colbost Croft Museum

On B884, 4 miles from Dunvegan, Colbost, Skye.

A museum in a blackhouse, containing 19th-century implements and furniture with a peat fire burning throughout the day. Replica of an illicit whisky still.

Open Apr-Oct, daily 10.00-18.30.

Explanatory displays. Car and coach parking. Group concessions. £.

Tel: 01470 521296   Email: Anniemac@annemacaskil.u-net.com

Corgarff Castle

Off A939, 10 miles NW of Ballater, Corgarff, Aberdeenshire.

Corgarff Castle is a fine 16th-century tower house, white-washed and restored, with later pavilions and star-shaped outworks. The castle was torched in 1571 by Adam Gordon of Auchindoun, killing Margaret Campbell, wife of Forbes of Towie, and 26 others of her household. Corgarff was burnt again by Jacobites in 1689, then again in 1716, and for a third time in 1746.

  In 1748 the government bought Corgarff, and it was later used as a base to help stop illicit whisky distilling. One of the floors houses a restored barrack room and whisky still.

Open daily Apr-Sep daily 9.30-18.30, last ticket 18.00; open wknds only Oct-Mar, Sat 9.30-16.30, Sun 14.00-16.30, last ticket 16.00.

Short walk to castle. Exhibition. Gift shop. Car and coach parking. Group concessions. £.

Tel: 01975 651460

Gaelic Whiskies - Whisky Exhibition

On A851, 8 miles S of Broadford, Eilean Iarmain, Skye.

Based at the highland estate offices of Fearann Eilean Iarmain, The Gaelic Whiskies was set up by Gaelic enthusiast Sir Iain Noble in 1976. Its aim was to provide the Gaelic-speaking communities of the Hebrides with a traditional malt whisky. The company has since flourished and now exports to countries such as Canada and Japan. Principle brands are the international award-winning Tè Bheag blend and Poit Dhubh, a fine premium malt. Small display of whisky-related artefacts. Outstanding views to Isle Ornsay, with its lighthouse, and the hills of the mainland beyond.

Open all year, Mon-Fri 9.00-17.30; Apr-Sep also Sat 10.30-14.30.

Free whisky tastings. Shop and exhibitions in gallery. Meals available in Hotel Eilean Iarmain next door.

Tel: 01471 833266   Fax: 01471 833260

Gordon & MacPhail Ltd

Boroughbriggs Road, Elgin IV30 1JY, Moray

Independent whisky bottler.

Tel: 01343 545111   Fax: 01343 540155

Loch Fyne Whiskies

Inveraray, Argyll.

Specialist whisky retailer. Whisky-related items. Mail order and twice-yearly newsletters.

Open all year, Mon-Sat 10.00-17.30, also Sun 12.30-17.00 Mar-Nov.

Tel: 01499 302219
Fax: 01499 302238   Web: www.lfw.co.uk

Moffat Wine Shop

8 Well Street, Moffat, Dumfriesshire.

Specialist whisky retailer with own malt 'The Corsleyburn' a 12-Year-Old triple distilled Lowland malt. Own-label malt whisky service, personalised for customers.

Open all year Mon-Sat 9.00-17.30.

Parking. Free tastings on Sat in season.

Tel: 01683 220554

Museum of Islay Life

Off A847, Port Charlotte, Islay.

Housed in an old church, this award-winning museum was opened in 1977 and covers all areas of island life. Displays include an important collection of carved stones, dating from the 6th to 16th centuries, as well as miniature reconstructions of prehistoric sites. There are also room exhibits, largely from Victorian times, and another item of interest is an illicit whisky still. There is a library and extensive archives.

Open Easter-Oct, Mon-Sat 10.00-16.30, Sun 14.00-16.30.

Explanatory displays. Sales area. WC. Disabled access (steps). Car and coach parking. £.

Tel: 01496 850358   Fax: 01496 850358

Royal Mile Whiskies

379-381 High Street, Edinburgh.

Specialist whisky retailer – over 300 malt whiskies ranging from £13.50 to £4000, dating from 1897 to the present day. Extensive range of international whisky and whiskey, as well as miniatures of Scottish beers and ales. Mail order available

Open all year, Mon-Sat 10.00-18.00, Sun 12.30-17.00; later hours in summer.

Tel: 0131 225 3383   Fax: 0131 226 2772   Email: keir@whiskies.demon.co.uk

Scotch Malt Whisky Society

87 Giles Street, Leith, Edinburgh EH6 6BZ.

Cask-strength bottlings and regular newsletter, tastings and whisky 'school'.

Tel: 0131 554 3451

Scotch Whisky Heritage Centre

Off A1, 354 Castlehill, Royal Mile, Edinburgh.

The Scotch Whisky Heritage centre is located beside Edinburgh Castle at the top of the Royal Mile and reveals the mystery of whisky making. The tour consists of four areas: area 1 explains Scotch whisky distilling, and through an audio-visual presentation the visitor is transported to a distillery in Scotland to learn how whisky is made. In area 2 the guides talk about Scotland's whisky regions and the general characteristics of the whisky produced. A model distillery allows the visitor to see the production processes, and there is an opportunity to nose a variety of whiskies. Area 3 introduces the centre's resident ghost: the former Master Blender, who explains about life in the whisky trade and the art of blending whisky. The fourth area takes the visitor on a barrel ride through 300 years of whisky history with life-like figures, background sounds and smells.

The tour takes fifty minutes, and concludes in the bar and bistro with a complimentary dram of blended whisky for adults and a discount voucher for a 70cl bottle of whisky in the centre shop. Children receive a soft drink and balloon.

Open daily 19.30-17.00; extended hours in summer; closed 25 Dec.

Guided tours available in eight languages: Dutch, English, French, German, Italian, Japanese, Portuguese and Spanish. Whisky Bond Bar and Bistro. Gift shop. WC. Disabled access. Corporate facilities and tutored whisky tastings also available. Group concessions. ££.

Tel: 0131 220 0441   Fax: 0131 220 6288

Email: enquiry@whisky-heritage.co.uk Web: www.whisky-heritage.co.uk

Signatory Vintage Scotch Whisky Co Ltd

7/8 Elizafield, Newhaven, Edinburgh EH6 5PY.

Independent whisky bottler.

Tel: 0131 555 4988   Fax: 0131 555 5211

Speyside Cooperage

Off A941, 2 miles NE of Aberlour, Dufftown Road, Craigellachie, Moray.

Speyside Cooperage is an award-winning working cooperage, with a unique visitor centre, where coopers and their apprentices repair oak casks for the whisky industry. Each year the cooperage repairs around 100,000 casks – barrels, hogsheads, butts and puncheons – many of which will be used to mature different whiskies. There is also the 'Acorn to Cask' exhibition, audio-visual presentation, tasting room, and a gift shop selling a range of goods crafted from wood.

Open all year: Easter-Sep, Mon-Sat 9.30-16.30, last admission Fri & Sat 16.00; Oct-Mar, Mon-Fri 9.30-16.30; closed Christmas & New Year. Coach parties welcome by appt.

Exhibition. Audio-visual presentation. Viewing gallery. Tastings. Gift shop. Picnic area. WC. Disabled WC and access to viewing gallery only. Car and coach parking. £.

Tel: 01340 871108   Fax: 01340 881437

Email: info@speyside-cooper.demon.co.uk

Whisky Castle

Main Street, Tomintoul.

Specialist whisky retailer, features vast array of miniatures, blends, malts, liqueurs. Collectors corner. On whisky trail, adjacent to the Highland Market.

Open Oct-Mar, Mon-Sat 9.00-18.00; May-Sep, Mon-Sat 9.00-21.00, Sun 12.30-17.30.

Parking nearby.

Tel: 01807 580213

Index